LUTHERAN QUARTERLY BOOKS

Editor, Paul Rorem, Princeton Theological Seminary
Associate Editors, Timothy Wengert, The Lutheran Theological Seminary at Philadelphia and Steven Paulson, Luther Seminary, St. Paul

Lutheran Quarterly Books will advance the same aims as *Lutheran Quarterly* itself, aims repeated by Theodore G. Tappert when he was editor fifty years ago and renewed by Oliver K. Olson when he revived the publication in 1987. The original four aims continue to grace the front matter and to guide the contents of every issue, and can now also indicate the goals of *Lutheran Quarterly Books:* "to provide a forum (1) for the discussion of Christian faith and life on the basis of the Lutheran confession; (2) for the application of the principles of the Lutheran church to the changing problems of religion and society; (3) for the fostering of world Lutheranism; and (4) for the promotion of understanding between Lutherans and other Christians."

For further information, see www.lutheranquarterly.com.

The symbol and motto of *Lutheran Quarterly,* VDMA for *Verbum Domini Manet in Aeternum* (1 Peter 1:25), was adopted as a motto by Luther's sovereign, Frederick the Wise, and his successors. The original "Protestant" princes walking out of the imperial Diet of Speyer 1529, unruly peasants following Thomas Muentzer, and from 1531 to 1547 the coins, medals, flags, and guns of the Smalcaldic League all bore the most famous Reformation slogan, the first Evangelical confession: the Word of the Lord remains forever.

V|D
M|A *Lutheran Quarterly Books*

Titles

> *Living by Faith: Justification and Sanctification*
>   by Oswald Bayer (2003)

Forthcoming

> *Harvesting Luther's Reflections on Theology, Ethics, and the Church,*
> essays from *Lutheran Quarterly* edited by Timothy Wengert, with
> foreword by David Steinmetz (fall 2003).

> *A More Radical Gospel: Essays on Eschatology, Authority, Atone-*
> *ment, and Ecumenism* by Gerhard O. Forde, edited by Mark
> Mattes and Steven Paulson (spring 2004).

LIVING *by* FAITH

Justification and Sanctification

OSWALD BAYER

Translated by
Geoffrey W. Bromiley

William B. Eerdmans Publishing Company
Grand Rapids, Michigan / Cambridge, U.K.

© 2003 Wm. B. Eerdmans Publishing Co.

Wm. B. Eerdmans Publishing Co.
255 Jefferson Ave. S.E., Grand Rapids, Michigan 49503 /
P.O. Box 163, Cambridge CB3 9PU U.K.

Printed in the United States of America

08 07 06 05 04 03   7 6 5 4 3 2 1

Library of Congress Cataloging-in-Publication Data

Bayer, Oswald.
[Aus Glauben Leben. English]
Living by faith: justification and sanctification /
Oswald Bayer; translated by Geoffrey W. Bromiley.
p.   cm.   — (Lutheran quarterly books)
Includes bibliographical references and indexes.
ISBN 0-8028-3987-8 (pbk.: alk. paper)
1. Justification (Christian theology).   2. Sanctification — Christianity.
3. Lutheran Church — Doctrines.   I. Title.   II. Series.

BT764.3.B3913   2003
234′.7 — dc21

2003044358

www.eerdmans.com

Contents

CONTENTS

Contents

Foreword

To begin this new Eerdmans series of *Lutheran Quarterly Books* with Oswald Bayer's strong word on justification by faith is not only fitting but also a pleasure. *Living by Faith: Justification and Sanctification* precisely fits the longstanding aims of *Lutheran Quarterly,* and it is always a pleasure to work with Oswald Bayer.

    Lutheran Quarterly Books will advance the same aims as *Lutheran Quarterly* itself, aims repeated by Theodore G. Tappert when he was editor fifty years ago and renewed by Oliver K. Olson when he revived the publication in 1987. The original four aims continue to grace the front matter and to guide the contents of every issue, and can now also indicate the goals of *Lutheran Quarterly Books:* "to provide a forum (1) for the discussion of Christian faith and life on the basis of the Lutheran confession; (2) for the application of the principles of the Lutheran church to the changing problems of religion and society; (3) for the fostering of world Lutheranism; and (4) for the promotion of understanding between Lutherans and other Christians."

    As editor of *Lutheran Quarterly,* I will serve as General Editor of the book series, joined by Associate Editors Timothy J. Wengert, successor to Tappert (and Olson) at the Lutheran Seminary in Philadelphia, and Steven Paulson, who teaches systematic theology at Luther Seminary in St. Paul. For the launching of this series we are grateful first of all to the Board of Directors, staff, authors, donors, and subscribers to *Lutheran Quarterly* who have carried this periodical through the perilous waters of independent theological publishing, and now most specifically to Wm. B. Eerdmans, Jr., for his interest in books on Lutheran history and theology. Appearing just after this Bayer book is a volume of *Lutheran Quarterly* essays by various authors on Martin Luther's basic teachings, edited by Timothy Wengert. Following shortly thereafter will be a collection of essays by Gerhard Forde, studies of the theology and music of Luther and J. S. Bach by Robin Leaver, and other monographs and collected essays. For general information about *Lutheran Quarterly,* visit our website at www.lutheranquarterly.com or contact the managing editor, Pastor Virgil Thompson, at 2715 S. Ray St., Spokane, WA 99223 (1-800-555-3813).

This monograph by Oswald Bayer, originally *Aus Glauben Leben: Über Rechtfertigung und Heiligung* (Stuttgart: Calwer, 1990 [2nd ed.]), is Bayer's first book in English. His many essays, however, have often been translated, including a dozen in *Lutheran Quarterly,* and have already introduced him to some English readers. As a Tübingen systematician, he engages the classical texts, particularly those of Martin Luther and Johann Georg Hamann, in order to draw upon their wealth and show their relevance in contemporary theological debate. His distinctively Lutheran emphasis on God's Word of Promise (see his *Promissio,* second edition 1989) is discussed in a *Lutheran Quarterly* essay (*LQ* 14 [2000]: 21-50) by Christine Helmer, who also there added a bibliography of Bayer's books and the essays available in English. Some of Bayer's essays and perhaps another monograph will appear in future volumes of *Lutheran Quarterly Books.*

For the appearance of this volume in English, the editor and author alike are grateful for the permission granted by Calwer Verlag and for the rendition by the venerable Geoffrey W. Bromiley, whose many contributions to Eerdmans translations include Ernst Käsemann's magisterial *Commentary on Romans* (1980). We also thank Amy Marga, Ph.D. candidate at Princeton Theological Seminary, especially for work on the endnotes so that they now include English editions of the works cited.

In this volume, Bayer probes Luther's theology, notably his Prefaces to the Bible, for the "incomparable breadth and depth" of the doctrine of justification. Contrary to most contemporary presentations, including the 1999 Lutheran and Roman Catholic "Joint Declaration on the Doctrine of Justification," Bayer does not consider justification to be one doctrinal theme among others. Alluding to Romans 4, Bayer maintains that justification has to do with everything, from creation out of nothing to the eschatological raising of the dead. Contemporary ecumenical dialogue needs this voice, since the recent statements have not resolved the old questions of how justification relates to sanctification, for example, or to ecclesiology.

We at *Lutheran Quarterly* thus offer this first volume of our new series in the hope and trust that it will further the periodical's traditional aims, as restated above. May the volume and the series serve those who live by faith in the God whose strong and promising Word creates out of nothing, justifies the ungodly, and raises the dead.

Paul Rorem
series editor

Preface to the First German Edition (1984)

"Living by faith" is the programmatic formula of Paul in Romans 1:17 that will be expounded in the pages that follow. It condenses not merely the epistle to the Romans but the whole of the apostle's theology, and indeed the message of the Bible as a whole. But what does it mean to live by faith? By the faith that God's all-powerful Word creates and imparts?

Those who try to answer this question can learn from Martin Luther. As he himself tells us, the gates of paradise opened for him when the truth of this formula disclosed itself to him and he recognized that the righteousness of faith consists solely in the fact that we are justified by the Word of God and with it have "forgiveness of sins and life and salvation."

There appears to be a general awareness in the worlds of church and theology that justification by faith alone is the center of Luther's Reformation theology. But this appearance is deceptive. Since neither the breadth nor the depth of justification by faith alone is really understood, it is thus impossible to comprehend that it is truly the center. When the Pauline and Reformation doctrine of justification is passed on without being understood, when it has become merely an empty formula, then we need not be surprised that it is passed on with some embarrassment, and with an apologetic tone. Thus comes the anxious question whether justification has anything to say to our contemporaries, who are allegedly inquiring, not for the grace of God, but rather, supposedly more radically, for the very existence of God.

The aim of this tractate is not to apologize for the doctrine of justification but to take it seriously in its incomparable breadth and depth.

The theme of justification is not one theme among many. It has principal significance. It touches on every theme. Justification concerns not merely one's own history, not only world history, but also natural history. It has to do with everything.

Hence sanctification is not something that follows justification. Instead, its theme is also none other than justification. Along these lines the fifth chapter ("Faith and Sanctification") refers primarily to the problem of the relation between the two, as it emerges in the later Melanchthon. Indeed, Pietism and Methodism laid such emphasis upon sanctification that the Reformation understanding of justification was more or less obscured.

To bring light into this obscurity, and thereby to meet critically the related problems of the modern mental and spiritual situation, it is helpful to learn from Luther. The following exposition of the Pauline formula "living by faith" is consistently oriented to texts of Luther, that great commentator upon Paul. It is thus also an introduction to Luther's own theology.

As a source our preference goes to Luther's Prefaces to the Bible. We shall thus draw attention especially to these texts that are usually neglected in the exposition of Luther's theology. Like the Catechisms and his hymns, these texts summarize Luther's theological work. Two other texts that are essential for this exposition will be found in the appendix.

[. . .] My wife took a greater part in this work than in previous projects; without her patience and constant criticism I could never even have begun, let alone finished, this tractate. I dedicate it to our children, who have shown such understanding for their father's work.

Oswald Bayer
Tübingen, July 14, 1984

Preface to the English Edition

Nearly twenty years ago, when this book was first published, the aftermath of the atheism debate had left behind the fact that greater importance was assigned to the question of God's existence than to that of God's grace. The problems of the Reformation period seemed outdated. Today, the emphasis of the theological debate has shifted, without the former questions having really been solved, which does not make things easier. In our times, it is not so much atheism that is on the agenda but the return of new — often polytheistic — types of religion. Simultaneously, the topic of "Law and Gospel" has changed its appearance. Our contemporaries, speaking generally, do not experience the law as *God's* law but rather as *anonymous* law, or in the best of cases, as "categorical imperative."

Nevertheless, in this and in other modern recastings and debates of our situation before God, there always remains the inescapable obligation that marks every person, an obligation that then becomes fatal if law and gospel are merged and not distinguished. In my view, the basic topic of justification and faith that reaches deeper than the paradigm shifts of the last decades is so fundamental that it is valid not only for the sixteenth or the twentieth century, but also for our new century and the times to come. It is the fundamental question of our being and our relation to God, the other, and the world.

When the article on justification, as suggested in this tractate, is understood in a sense so broad and deep as to encompass even creation and the eschaton, then it does not suffice to speak of this article merely as the *articulus stantis et cadentis ecclesiae,* the article upon which the *church* stands or falls. It is the being of the world and its relation to God that hinge upon justification. *Creatio ex nihilo* (creation out of nothing), the basis of the Jewish and Christian doctrine of creation, is to be understood in terms of the theology of justification — and vice versa. God is obliged neither to create and preserve the world nor to forgive sin. Everything that exists is the result of pure goodness, "and all this is done out of pure, fatherly, and divine goodness and mercy, without any merit or worthiness of mine at all," as Luther states in his explanation of the first (!) article of the Apostles' Creed.

When this ontological significance of justification is grasped,[1] then it becomes clear that justification is neither merely an event in the interior of the believer nor one among many ways to express what Christian faith is about. The 1999 "Joint Declaration on the Doctrine of Justification" has failed to appreciate this breadth and depth, and has thus blurred the whole topic. Ecumenical discourse is to be welcomed — but not at the price of mistaking justification as just one *façon de parler* among others.

Last but not least, the ontological breadth and depth of justification raises the question of God's own righteousness: the question of suffering and of the end to all evil. The outline of a Lutheran dogmatics offered here is oriented towards the eschatological removal of the terrible hiddenness of God and God's righteousness. Those who have faith do not close their eyes to injustice and suffering, yet they do not give them the last word, but rather lament and live against them — by faith.

I wish to express my deep gratitude to Professor Paul Rorem of Princeton Theological Seminary and to the publisher, William B. Eerdmans, Jr. Without their encouragement and their appreciation of specific features of German language and theology, this book could have been neither translated nor published.

Oswald Bayer
Tübingen, May 23, 2002

---

1. Cf. Oswald Bayer, "The Doctrine of Justification and Ontology," *Neue Zeitschrift für Systematische Theologie und Religionsphilosophie* 43:2 (2001): 44-53.

Chapter One

In the Dispute of "Justifications"

Who Am I?

Those who justify themselves are under compulsion to do so. There is no escape. We cannot reject the question that others put to us: Why have you done this? What were you thinking about? Might you not have done something else? In the other's view of us, and also in our own view, we always find ourselves to be the ones who are already being questioned and who have to answer. Complaints are made against us. We are forced to justify ourselves, and as we do so, we usually want to be right. Before the court of law, what constitutes our whole life is disclosed with particular clarity. The world of the court is not a special world of its own, but just a particular instance — a very striking one — of what is being done always and everywhere.

There is no escaping the questions and evaluations of others. If one accepts and welcomes the other or not, if one greets the other or not, if one acknowledges the other — either through praise or reproach, affirmation or negation — or if one does not acknowledge the other and regards the other as worthless, a decision is made concerning our being or non-being. Only a being that is recognized and acknowledged is a being that is alive. If no one were to call and greet me by name, if no one were ready to speak to me and look at me, then I would be socially nonexistent. I would even be physically nonexistent, I would have no life at all, if my parents had not acknowledged me and respected my life even before my birth. I would no longer have any life if after my birth my parents had not smiled at me and talked to me, thus opening a space for community, accepting and acknowledging me. An unwanted child is aware of this rejection. The denial of unconditional and anticipated recognition, the denial of love, shows how necessary recognition is. Its denial is a painful and especially impressive indication of its necessity, its necessity for life.

We want constant recognition of ourselves because it is vitally necessary. We need its confirmation and renewal. If it is lacking, we try to regain it or even to coerce it. We want to produce something which others will say gives pleasure and ought to be recognized, so that it is rewarded by a glance or a word, and thus finds an answer.

To be recognized and justified; to cause ourselves to be justified or to justify ourselves in attitude, thought, word, and action; to need to justify our being; or simply to be allowed to exist without needing to justify our being — all this makes for our happiness or unhappiness and is an essential part of our humanity.

We are rational creatures. This means that we are addressed; we therefore can hear and answer. But we thereby do have to hear, to answer, to give an account of ourselves. In this regard we are always social creatures. I can only hear and address *another* person, and hear and address myself only in a derived way. Entering into dialogue with myself, engaging in an inner monologue, in thinking, is possible only on the presupposition of language by which mutual recognition and justification occur. As social beings we live by the word given and heard. This word either grants or denies us recognition and justification.

This basic human feature has been particularly intensified in modern times and has given rise to ruthless questioning and complaining.[1] With what right do you exist at all, rather than not exist? With what right do you exist the way you do and not some other way? Pressured by such questions, we must all submit the authorization of our existence to the proof. We must inexorably offer persuasive reasons for our right to exist

1. Odo Marquard, "Der angeklagte und der entlastete Mensch," *Abschied vom Prinzipiellen, Philosophische Studien*, No. 7724 (2) (Stuttgart: Reclams Universalbibliothek, 1984), 50f. Translated under the title *Farewell to Matters of Principle: Philosophical Studies* (New York: Oxford University Press, 1989). Marquard is paraphrased fairly literally in the following passage.

and to exist the way we are. Our whole life histories are placed before a permanent tribunal in which we act as accused, prosecutor, and judge. Throughout our lives we continually seek to find excuses for the fact that we live as we do, that we are existent rather than nonexistent, and that we are as we are and not something different.

The French Revolution offers us a striking example of the obsessive use of tribunals. Germany too, with its total moralization, has provided less painful yet occasionally deadly examples since 1968. The excessive subjection of people's lives to tribunals is seen since the French Revolution in Stalinism, National Socialism, and in those political contexts in which the socially formed conscience is expected to accuse itself in order to receive collective absolution. In such cases the subjection of human reality to tribunals is particularly crude and monstrous. In a milder and less noticeable way, however, the same thing occurs among smaller groups, and also in the field of advertising, for instance, when a homemaker is supposed to have a bad conscience if she does not use the right brand of cleanser. Television advertising depicts the self-accusation of a wife or mother when her conscience reproaches her for not using the right softener.

Constantly having to justify and fulfill oneself, or, on the other hand, finding freedom from this urge or pressure, affects the individual's relationship to the self, in which it cannot exist but through relationship to others. There is no such thing as an autocratic individual, totally independent of the surrounding world and its recognition. The individual is always socially formed. It is self-consciousness as it has formed itself and continues to be formed in the process of mutual recognition. Striving to find approval in the eyes of others, being noticed and not being dismissed as nothing by others, demonstrates that I cannot relate to myself without relating to the world. It applies to our social birth as well as our physical birth. I constantly vacillate, even to the very end of life, between the judgment others make about me and my own judgment of myself. I am constantly trying to ascertain others' judgment about me and my own judgment of myself; I arrive at some point of calm, and then become unsure of myself again. My identity is a floating one. Who am I? asked Dietrich Bonhoeffer.[2] Am I what others say about

2. Dietrich Bonhoeffer, "Wer bin ich?" in *Widerstand und Ergebung. Briefe und Auf-*

me? Am I what I know about myself? Am I balanced between these different evaluations? Questions such as these relate to my inner being, not just to something external. They affect the core, not the shell. It is not true that judgment is an addition to being. What I am, I am in my judgment about myself, intertwined with the judgment made of me by others. Person is a "forensic term."[3]

World History as a Battle for Mutual Recognition

As it is in my own life history, so it is in world history, of which my history is a part. We should speak more cautiously and soberly in the plural, of world histories: namely, the histories of great social groups or movements; the histories of alliances, nations, and blocs; histories which stand apart and never merge into a world history in the singular. These world histories are nothing but the histories of the seeking, enforcing, denying, or lacking of mutual recognition. They are the histories of vindications and of the assigning of guilt. They are one long story of the battle for mutual recognition, a life and death battle. In this regard, then, we can indeed speak of a world history in the singular.

Predominant in this dispute is the problematic relationship of power, rights, and justice. We see this, for example, in the dispute between the Athenians and the defeated Melians that Thucydides stylized as a common human experience in his history of the Peloponnesian war: "In human negotiations, there is justice only when both opponents are under

---

zeichnungen aus der Haft, vol. 8 of *Dietrich Bonhoeffer Werke,* ed. Christian Gremmels, Eberhard Bethge, et al. (Gütersloh: Christian Kaiser Verlag, 1998), 513f. Translated under the title, "Who am I?" in *Letters and Papers from Prison,* 3rd edition (New York: Macmillan, 1972), 347ff.; cf. Oswald Bayer, "Wer bin ich? Gott als Autor meiner Lebensgeschichte," *Theologische Beiträge* 11 (1980): 245-61. Translated under the title "God as Author of My Life-History," *Lutheran Quarterly* 2 (1988): 437-56.

3. John Locke, "Of Ideas," Book 2, Chapter 27 ("Of Identity and Diversity"), Paragraph 26, *An Essay Concerning Human Understanding,* vol. 2 of *The Works of John Locke* (Aalen: Scientia, 1963), 69. Locke says that "person" is a "forensic term." The word "forensic" derives from the Latin *forum,* the public square where trials were held, and applies to the judge's sentence.

the same force, while superiors impose whatever is possible and the weak acquiesce."[4] This experience is as true today as it was in antiquity. Thomas Hobbes, the translator of Thucydides, is of the same mind. In the battle for justifications, the two extremes of despotism and anarchy alternate. The struggle for mutual recognition will often come to a temporary halt; Diderot foresaw this in 1774 as the outcome of the French Revolution: A strong man will emerge who will "tell those who up to that moment believed themselves to be everything that they are nothing, and they will say, we are nothing. He will tell them that he is their lord, and they will unanimously respond, you are our lord. He will tell them under what conditions he is ready to subject them, and they will accept them."[5]

History of Nature: Chain of Guilt or Causality?

Not just our own history, nor even world history, but all earthly being, including natural history, might be seen as a battle for mutual recognition, as a problem of justification, justice, and righteousness. As the ecological crisis has shown us, this is in any case true about our own relationship with our fellow creatures and their relationship with us. In Romans 8:20f., Paul speaks about our guilt in enslaving, exploiting, and suppressing nature, and about our violence to creatures unwillingly subjected to our nothingness and injustice. Those who agree with Paul recognize a right of nature and their own responsibility as "duty-bound to nature."[6]

Anaximander of Miletus is even more radical than Paul when refer-

4. Thukydides, *Geschichte des Peloponnesischen Krieges,* in *Die Bibliothek der Alten Welt [Griechische Reihe],* ed. Walter Rüegg (Zürich/Stuttgart: Artemis-Verlag, 1960), V, 89, p. 433. Translated by Steven Lattimore under the title *The Peloponnesian War* (Indianapolis: Hackett, 1998), 295 (translation altered).

5. Denis Diderot as quoted by Reinhart Koselleck, "Vergangene Zukunft der frühen Neuzeit," *Vergangene Zukunft. Zur Semantik geschichtlicher Zeiten* (1979; Frankfurt am Main: Suhrkamp Verlag, 1995), 36f. Translated by Keith Tribe under the title *Futures Past: On the Semantics of Historical Time* (Cambridge, MA: MIT Press, 1985), 13 (translation altered).

6. "Pflichtträger der Natur." Johann G. Hamann, *Golgotha und Scheblimini! Von einem Prediger in der Wüsten,* vol. 3 of *Sämtliche Werke,* ed. Josef Nadler (Wien: Thomas-Morus-Presse im Verlag Herder, 1951), 299, 15.

ring to the community of justice to which all things belong. In a fragment that is the oldest extant text in Western philosophy, deriving from a time in which all philosophy was philosophy of nature, he says, "The source from which existing things derive their existence is also that to which they return at their destruction, according to necessity; for they give justice and make reparation to one another for their injustice, according to the arrangement of time."[7] This statement implies a different understanding of nature from that of Stoicism with its view of the *logos,* all the more from our modern schema of causality, the law of cause and effect. According to Anaximander the world consists of mutual address and response, and therefore of responsibility; in the language of judgment he speaks of "justice" and "reparation." Thus the nexus of the world as a whole, all nature, consists of such a "forensic"[8] process. The cosmic and moral orders have not yet separated from each other.[9] The cosmic order is perceived to be one of linguistic communication. At a later time "guilt" will be changed into "cause." The similies in the language of judgment fade and become abstract concepts which serve to formulate the "laws of nature," and these are distinguished from the laws of morality and the laws of history. For Anaximander, however, the physical order is simultaneously a moral order and a forensic order.

We cannot conceive of a just world order apart from the thought of judgment. In this point, traditions as diverse as Greek antiquity and ancient Israel come together. In the various traditions of the wisdom of Greece, Israel, and surrounding nations, this feeling about the cosmos has come down to us, and it should make us think, precisely because of its diversity.

The wisdom of Israel leads us to the decisive point. The important thing is to see the theological, in the strict sense of the term, dimension of

7. Anaximander, No. B,1, in *Die Fragmente der Vorsokratiker, griechisch und deutsch,* ed. Hermann Diels and Walther Kranz (Berlin: Weidmann, 1951). Translated and edited by Kathleen Freeman under the title *Ancilla to the pre-Socratic philosophers: a complete translation of the fragments in Diels, Fragmente der Vorsokratiker* (Oxford: Blackwell, 1948), 19.

8. See note 3.

9. Cf. *Frieden mit der Natur,* ed. Klaus Michel Meyer-Abich (Freiburg: Herder, 1979), 30f. [editor's introduction]. On Heraclitus, see Hans Welzel, *Naturrecht und materiale Gerechtigkeit,* 4th edition (Göttingen: Vandenhoeck & Ruprecht, 1980), 9f.

the problem of justification. The dispute of the "justifications" does not come to a halt in the presence of God.

God in the Dispute of the "Justifications"

The book of Job, a book of the wisdom of Israel, illustrates the fact that life is not lived in anonymous causality but involves address and answer.[10] This dialogue can even reach the point of our calling upon God and demanding that he should justify himself: "Let the Almighty answer me."[11] There is a link from Job to many modern forms of atheism, for they too function in the context of that dialogue, being questioned and having to justify themselves.

Justification, justice, judgment, righteousness — these are not only the leading terms in the multi-layered process of the tradition of Israel with all its dissonance (as in the controversy between Job and his friends). They are not only leading terms in a process of tradition that might have come to its reconciling conclusion in the New Testament and would only produce as an after-effect a specialized religious vocabulary of explicit biblical exposition. Rather, these terms tell those contemporaries whose eyes are open to the phenomena just what the nexus of the world truly is, namely, no nexus at all, but foremost an embattled and lacerated world in which creation is "rent and torn from top to bottom."[12] There is no agreement, no harmony in the world. It rings out

10. Cf. the core of Luther's theology: "For God does not deal, nor has he ever dealt, with man otherwise than through a word of promise. We in turn cannot deal with God otherwise than through faith in the Word of his promise." Martin Luther, *The Babylonian Captivity of the Church* (1520), *Luther's Works* (hereafter cited as LW), American Edition, 55 vols., ed. J. Pelikan and H. Lehmann (St. Louis and Philadelphia: Concordia and Fortress, 1955ff.), 36:42; translation slightly altered (*Luthers Werke* [hereafter cited as WA], 60 vols., ed. J. F. Knaake et al. [Weimar: Böhlau, 1883-1996], 6, 516, 30-32).

11. Job 31:35.

12. See Georg Büchner, *Dantons Tod* in *Dantons Tod oder Die Trauerarbeit im Schönen: ein Theater-Lesebuch,* ed. Peter von Becker (Frankfurt am Main: Syndikat, 1980), Act III, par. 382, p. 51. Translated by Hedwig Rappolt under the title *Danton's Death* (New York: TSL, 1980), 167.

like "cracked bells."[13] For this reason the issue of theodicy, of vindicating God, arises.[14] Can God, and talk about God, be justified in the face of evil and suffering? Is there not injustice in God?[15]

It has surely become plain to us that the word "justification" is utilized in many different realms. We have seen that it points to our own lives, then to world history, then to natural history. In sum, it points to our human history with God, and this is far from unequivocal.

These varied histories do not have a total meaning that we can easily discern, that can be provisionally assumed or — even with the forethought that it might be revised — hypothetically demonstrated. Instead, they must be viewed as a chain of justifications in which the struggle for mutual recognition rages and finally reaches the point in the Psalms and Job where God himself is challenged to justify himself and thus to achieve recognition: "So that you are justified in your sentence and blameless when you will be judged."[16] God enters into controversy with the nations,[17] with Israel,[18] and with individuals like Job. Today we have a different forum of judgment. Gottfried W. Leibniz and Immanuel Kant judge the cause of God and his justice at the forum of reason. This is how they reach their decision. In G. W. F. Hegel's philosophy of world history the justification of God is found in history. World history is world judgment.[19]

13. Georg Büchner, *Woyzeck,* in *Goethes Urfaust, Büchners Woyzeck,* edited and compiled by Friedrich Dürrenmatt (Zürich: Verlag der Arche, 1980), Bild 21, p. 187. Translated and edited by Edward McInnes under the title *Woyzeck* (Glasgow: University of Glasgow French and German Publications, 1991).

14. From the Greek *theos* (God) and *dike* (debate about rights, lawsuit).

15. See Rom. 3:5, "That God is unjust to inflict wrath on us?" and 9:14, "What then are we to say? Is there injustice on God's part?"

16. See Ps. 51:4. The important passive formulation that Luther follows in his theology, "when you will be judged," does not follow the Masoretic text, but the Septuagint.

17. Cf. Jer. 25:31.

18. Cf. Hos. 12:3 and Mic. 6:2.

19. Georg Wilhelm Friedrich Hegel, *Grundlinien der Philosophie des Rechts,* 4th ed., Philosophische Bibliothek, vol. 124a, ed. Johannes Hoffmeister (Hamburg: Meiner, 1955) §340ff., pp. 288ff. Translated by T. M. Knox under the title *Hegel's Philosophy of Right* (Oxford: Clarendon Press, 1942), §340ff., pp. 215ff.

Chapter Two

The Lawsuit about God
before the Court of Human Reason

The theme of justification is not one special theme, such that there might be other themes alongside it. It embraces the totality. All reality is involved in the justification debate. There can be no denying this. None of us can escape it. We are not consulted as to whether we would like to live in it or not. Even suicide,[1] which is sometimes called free or voluntary death on the view that — at least in this unique point — there was (is?) freedom, endorses the structure of justification. For often suicide relates to a balancing of life. The term itself shows that those who commit it are "judging themselves." Even this final act takes place within the structure of justification and judgment.

In this context of justification, it is not logically necessary to speak of God, less so today than ever. The general orientations articulated in philosophical and especially metaphysical thinking have been radically altered, as modern forms of atheism show. But the fact has not changed that the essential situations of our lives are situations of justification. Indeed, they have become unbearably sharper. From the time of Leibniz, the question of theodicy has become the key problem of our modern understanding of

1. Albert Camus, *The Myth of Sisyphus and Other Essays,* trans. Justin O'Brien (New York: Alfred A. Knopf, 1955), 3. Originally published as *Le Mythe de Sisyphe. Essai sur l'absurde* (Paris: Gallimard, 1942), 16: "There is but one truly serious philosophical problem and that is suicide. Judging whether life is or is not worth living amounts to answering the fundamental question of philosophy. All the rest . . . comes afterward."

9

the world and even of our world relationship, that is, the key problem not only of reflection on experience, but of experience itself, and therefore of life ("Lebenswelt") itself. Now that the question of theodicy has been secularized, humanity is inescapably and totally burdened with judgment. The consequences are fatal, which all try to evade. The well-known mechanisms of exoneration are the result, whereby we always say that others are in the wrong, never ourselves.

Facing this tribunal, we finally have to justify, and continually to question, our whole existence. We are always called upon to legitimate our existence. We have to demonstrate each moment that we deserve to exist, to be noted, addressed, welcomed, and honored, even if it is by contradiction. As Friedrich Engels said concerning modern history, we must all "justify our existence before the judgment seat of reason or relinquish our existence."[2]

The modern problem of justification is a secularization of the old question of Job. To understand our situation we must go back to that question.

The dispute of justifications reaches its climax in the theodicy lawsuit about God. Why do the just have to suffer?[3] Why does God not resist evil? Why does God not intervene? Why does God seem not to care? Why does God evade us? "My God, my God, why have you forsaken me?"[4]

Why? This question, this lament, is an open wound that hurts. There is a primal human impulse to close this wound. That impulse wants to provide the conclusive answer to the unavoidable question raised by that wound, the metaphysical question about the ground of the world with its accompanying orderliness. The impulse expects such an answer from the "one ground" and its goodness.

Two types of answers might be given that differ from one another.

---

2. Karl Marx and Friedrich Engels, *Werke,* vol. 20 (Berlin: Dietz, 1962), 16.
3. Cf. Jer. 12:1: "Righteous art thou, O LORD, when I complain to thee; yet I would plead my case before thee. Why does the way of the wicked prosper? Why do all who are treacherous thrive?"
4. See Ps. 22:1.

The one involves contemplative thinking — let us call it "contemplative theodicy." The other consists of action; we call it "active theodicy."

Contemplative Theodicy

For Plato, tragedy's experience of suffering was unbearable, so he invoked the unity of a good ground and a good conclusion by claiming that God never does what is evil and always does what is good.[5] In the last resort suffering is only an appearance. "The god is blameless."[6] For Augustine, too, suffering and contradiction in detail do not refute the total order. "The whole is greater than the part."[7] This is still a decisive argument for Leibniz, who establishes the modern form of questioning. In his 1710 *Essais de Théodicée* he discusses the goodness of God, human freedom, and the origin of evil. "Metaphysical evil consists of simple imperfection, physical evil is suffering, and moral evil is sin."[8] God permits evil, so that out of it comes good. The imperfection of the part contributes to the greater perfection of the whole.

Hegel expressly refers to the thinking of Leibniz. According to Hegel's philosophy of world history, the justification of God lies in history. "Our approach is thus far a theodicy, a justification of God such as Leibniz in his own way attempted metaphysically in still abstract and indefinite categories. The evil *(das Übel)* in the world, wickedness *(das Böse)* included, ought to be grasped (as meaningful), the thinking spirit ought to be reconciled with what is negative. And it is in world history

5. Plato, *Politeia,* ed. Otfried Höffe (Berlin: Akademie Verlag, 1997), 397a; 383c [*typoi peri theologias*]. Translated by A. D. Lindsay under the title *The Republic* (New York: Knopf, 1992), 56-61.

6. Plato, *Politeia,* 617e, cf. 379b; *The Republic,* 306-7, cf. 56.

7. "Magis enim est totum quam pars." Augustine, *De Immortalitate Animae,* 7, 12 in *Patrologia Latina,* ed. J. P. Migne (Paris: Migne, 1844-1864), 32, 1027. Translated by Gerard Watson under the title *Soliloquies and Immortality of the Soul* (Warminster: Aris & Phillips, 1990), 143.

8. Gottfried Wilhelm Leibniz, *Die Theodizee,* Philosophische Bibliothek, vol. 4., ed. A. Buchenau (Hamburg, Leipzig: Meiner, 1925), 110f. Translated by E. M. Huggard under the title *Theodicy Abridged,* ed. Diogenes Allen (Indianapolis: Bobbs-Merrill, 1966).

11

that the total mass of concrete evil is displayed."[9] On the basis of the incarnation and the death of God, world history is on the whole for Hegel capable of a rational understanding. Through what is negative, through death, the whole is justified as meaningful. The individual and the particular, however, will perish in the process. "Reason cannot tarry at the point at which some individuals have been offended."[10] "Truth is in the whole."[11]

Theodor Adorno reverses this saying of Hegel. For him all efforts to justify the whole by passing through what is negative are valueless. "The whole is untruth."[12] Although with an anti-metaphysical intention, the negative is again reshaped into a metaphysic. It is shaped into the concept of the "deepest essence" of total negativity that is antitypical to a "highest essence." In Adorno this negative concept of unity is linked to the hope of a negation of what is negative. This is a despairing hope, of course, which is no longer grounded in an impregnable belief in practical reason, as it is in Kant.

Active Theodicy

In his 1788 *Critique of Practical Reason* Kant lays the foundation for an answer to the theodicy question that we might describe as active theodicy. Following Kant, we cannot justify the goodness and righteousness of God by what we know from experience in this world.[13] We

9. G. W. F. Hegel, *Die Vernunft in der Geschichte* in *Vorlesungen über die Philosophie der Weltgeschichte,* Philosophische Bibliothek, vol. 171a, ed. J. Hoffmeister (Hamburg, Leipzig: Meiner, 1968), 48. Translated by Robert Hartman under the title *Reason in History* (New York: Liberal Arts Press, 1953); translation altered.

10. Hegel, *Die Vernunft in der Geschichte,* 48; cf. 76.

11. G. W. F. Hegel, *Phänomenologie des Geistes,* 6th ed., Philosophische Bibliothek, vol. 114, ed. Johannes Hoffmeister (Hamburg, Leipzig: Meiner, 1952), 21. Translated by A. V. Miller under the title *Phenomenology of Spirit* (Oxford: Clarendon Press, 1977), 11.

12. Theodor W. Adorno, *Minima Moralia: Reflexionen aus dem beschädigten Leben* (Frankfurt am Main: Suhrkamp Verlag, 1973), 57. Translated by E. F. N. Jephcott under the title *Minima Moralia: Reflections from a Damaged Life* (London: New Left Books, 1974).

13. Immanuel Kant, *Über das Mißlingen aller philosophischen Versuche in der Theodizee*

have to postulate them on the basis of moral resolution against worldly experience. A theodicy is legitimate, "authentic" in Kant's words, "if it is a pronouncement of the same reason through which we form our concept of God — necessarily prior to all experience — as a moral and wise being."[14] This is a matter, not for theoretical reason, but for "efficacious practical reason, which, just as in legislating it commands absolutely without further grounds, so it can be considered as the unmediated definition and voice of God through which he gives meaning to the letter of his creation."[15] According to Johann Gottlieb Fichte, the world is "the material of our duties."[16] The good will that is defined by the moral law, and that postulates the goodness and righteousness of God against worldly experience, offers by acting the only possible solution to the problem of theodicy.

God's "World Adventure"

Many Christians and non-Christians accept Kant's moral solution, though more in desperation than with rational certainty. Some also link it to Hegel's view that God needs humanity and its history to fulfill himself: "God needs humanity." Hans Jonas thinks of "God as committing himself to questionable human custody so as to achieve fulfillment, to be either saved or ruined by what man does with himself and the world." "The courses our lives take are like the lines on God's face." Because "God grows with the dreadfully ambivalent harvest of our deeds," the impression we make on God is

---

(1791), vol. 9 of *Werke in zehn Bänden,* ed. Wilhelm Weischedel (Darmstadt: Wissenschaftliche Buchgesellschaft, 1983), 114. Translated and edited by Allen Wood and George di Giovanni under the title "On the miscarriage of all philosophical trials in theodicy" in *Religion Within the Boundaries of Mere Reason and Other Writings* (Cambridge: Cambridge University Press, 1998), 23.

14. Kant, *Über das Mißlingen,* 116; "On the miscarriage," 24.

15. Kant, *Über das Mißlingen,* 116; "On the miscarriage," 24f.

16. Johann Gottlieb Fichte, *Sämtliche Werke,* vol. 3, ed. Immanuel H. Fichte (Bonn: Marcus [Berlin: Veit], 1965), 185.

for both good and evil. We can build and we can destroy, we can heal and we can wound, we can nourish the deity or leave it hungry, we can perfect its image or distort it. The scars of the one will be just as lasting as the radiance of the other. The immortality of our actions is thus no reason for empty pride. We had rather wish that most of our deeds would leave no traces. But this is not granted to us. They draw their lines, and these are permanent.[17]

This active — moral — answer to the theodicy question is not just a possibility of philosophical thinking nor is it held only by non-Christians. During the last four decades it has had a wide influence upon the work done by theology and the church. The Jewish thinker Jonas has combined it with a strong contemplative element by referring to God's "world adventure." In this adventure, God's entire being "is at stake" so that "in each inner-worldly act this risk is always present."

> After God has given himself totally to the developing world, he has nothing more to give. It is now up to humanity to give to God. We can do this when in the course of life we see to it that it never or seldom happens that what takes place must cause God to regret that he let the world come into being. This might well be the secret of the thirty-six righteous who in Jewish teaching will never be wanting in the world.[18]

Jonas himself describes the contemplative foundation and penetration of his moral answer to the theodicy question as a "myth," a "symbolic attempt that best expresses what seems to me to bring meaning into the riddle of being and existence." In saying this, Jonas is thinking about the ghastly event that goes by the name of Auschwitz. Jonas' own mother perished there. With "meaning," Jonas implies "nothing reconciling," even if

17. Hans Jonas, "Unsterblichkeit und heutige Existenz," *Zwischen Nichts und Ewigkeit* (Göttingen: Kleine Vandenhoeck Reihe [no. 165], 1963), 44-72, esp. 58. The texts being followed are on pp. 59f., 68, 71, 72, and are taken from *Reflexionen finsterer Zeit. Zwei Vorträge von Fritz Stern und Hans Jonas,* ed. Otfried Hofius (Tübingen: Mohr, 1984), 63-86.

18. For the thirty-six righteous, see Rudolf Mach, *Der Zaddik in Talmud und Midrasch* (Leiden: E. J. Brill, 1957), and R. Weisskopf, *Gematria: Buchstabenberechnung, Tora und Schöpfung im rabbinischen Judentum,* 2 vols. (Ph.D. diss., n.p., 1975), 53-81, esp. 69ff.

he insists on the "freedom of the spirit," that has to do "in the idea with the totality of everything." Even though we cannot see, we have to say that "while we cannot 'see' the whole, we can speak about its nature, basis, and destination."[19]

It is in this moving way that Jonas discusses and advocates the justification of God. He conducts the lawsuit about God in a way that is both contemplative and active.

Through Work to Play: Return to Paradise

The problem of justification in its modern form finds impressive treatment in Heinrich von Kleist's essay, "Über das Marionettentheater."[20] It tackles the question whether and how the gracefulness and charm that we have lost can be recaptured. Can art and culture lead us back to a second naïveté, back to nature, to our lost paradise?

The essay tells about a young man who was graceful and spontaneous until he saw that he was being observed and then began to observe himself. In the effort to recapture his graceful movement self-consciously, he discovered that he had lost both grace and spontaneity. Such a loss was "unavoidable since we ate of the tree of knowledge. Paradise is now sealed against us, and the cherub stands behind us. We must journey around the world and see whether perhaps the back door to paradise is open."[21] Kleist expects us to be able to return to nature through perfected cultural achievement, through education, and through work upon ourselves. His model here is the ballet artist whose performance conceals the fact that much toil and effort lie behind the apparently light and natural movements. The Latin word *gratia* means both grace and charm. Kleist's hope is that through extreme exertion and control we can attain once again to

19. Jonas, *Zwischen Nichts und Ewigkeit,* 22.

20. Heinrich von Kleist, *Über das Marionettentheater,* vol. 2 of *Sämtliche Werke und Briefe,* 7th ed., edited by Helmut Sembdner (München: Hanser, 1984), 338-45. Cf. Beate Günzler, "'Über das Marionettentheater', Kleists säkularisiertes Verständnis von Schöpfung, Sünde und Eschaton," *Neue Zeitschrift für Systematische Theologie* 32 (1990): 1-25.

21. Kleist, *Über das Marionettentheater,* 342.

the naturalness of the Being that is granted to us; gracefulness shall be earned.

This approach, which Kleist decisively corrected after his 1801 "Kant crisis,"[22] is not his alone. Friedrich Schiller found in "playing" a second recaptured naïveté. In his 1795 *On the Aesthetic Education of Man,*[23] he anticipates play as the epitome of the final state that is reached in the dialectic of the human cultural process in the tension between the sensory and the moral, between nature and law, between duty and inclination, between charm and dignity. Play does not precede work; it results from it. According to Kant, "Only after vanquishing monsters did Hercules become Musagetes, leader of the Muses."[24] "We must journey around the world and see whether perhaps the back door to paradise is open."

Kleist and Schiller expect even more from humanity than their teacher Kant; for him human existence justifies itself by the fulfillment of duty, by obedience to the law. For them the whole problem of culture is at stake, the relationship of human work and achievement to nature. Herbert Marcuse, one of the intellectual fathers of the student movement, attempted to take up this intention when in *Eros and Civilization,* under the concept of "play," he thought that the world of work would itself become erotic.[25] According to Marcuse, we have advanced so far technologically that we can now achieve a return to paradise. What has become second na-

22. Günzler, "Kleists säkularisiertes Verständnis," 3. Günzler says that Mr. C. in the *Marionettentheater* "stands for the rejection of belief in self-fulfillment and therefore represents Kleist's thinking after the Kant crisis, namely, that thought is unable to attain to reality through the world of appearance and phenomena."

23. See Friedrich Schiller, *Über die ästhetische Erziehung des Menschen in einer Reihe von Briefen,* comp. Wolfgang Düsing (München: Hanser, 1981). Edited and translated by Elizabeth M. Wilkinson and L. A. Willoughby under the title *On the Aesthetic Education of Man, in a Series of Letters* (Oxford: Clarendon, 1967).

24. Immanuel Kant, *Die Religion innerhalb der Grenzen der bloßen Vernunft* (1793), vol. 7 of *Werke in zehn Bänden,* ed. Wilhelm Weischedel (Darmstadt: Wissenschaftliche Buchgesellschaft, 1983), 670 [original in italics]. Translated by Theodore M. Greene and Hoyt H. Hudson under the title *Religion Within the Limits of Reason Alone* (New York: Harper, 1960), 19n.

25. Herbert Marcuse, *Eros and Civilization: A New Inquiry Into Freud* (Boston: Beacon, 1974 [1966]). Translated into German under the title "Triebstruktur und Gesellschaft," vol. 5 of *Herbert Marcuse Schriften* (Frankfurt am Main: Suhrkamp, 1979).

ture to us in our technological world can be superceded by a new birth, so that now for the first time we can live a life of "play," a life of freedom. We can now, he says, overcome the rigid one-dimensionality of technological rationality as Max Weber describes it. Marcuse seeks to oppose the reality principle of Sigmund Freud, namely, the thesis that culture is possible only by renunciation. His expectation of self-merited play, the result of human work, was the great vision that fascinated the student movement.

Atlas of the World

Even those who do not share Marcuse's solution to the modern problem of justification cannot overlook the fact that it is our specifically modern desire to achieve, by means of perfect performance and labor, what Karl Marx called "self-generation" of man: to move beyond our prehistory of misery and to move forward into what might be described as authentic history. Ernst Bloch concludes his *Principle of Hope* by saying that

> man everywhere is still living in prehistory, indeed all and everything still stands before the creation of the world, of a right world. *True genesis is not at the beginning but at the end,* and it starts to begin only when society and existence become radical, i.e. grasp their roots. But the root of history is the working, creating human being who reshapes and overhauls the given facts. Once he has grasped himself and established what is his, without expropriation and alienation, in real democracy, there arises in the world something which shines into the childhood of all and in which no one has yet been: homeland.[26]

We homeless ones are moving out of our state of misery, out of a foreign land, and coming back home, coming back to paradise. This will be the result of our work, of our perfected cultural achievement.

No one whose eyes are open can evade the claims made by Bloch

---

26. Ernst Bloch, *Das Prinzip Hoffnung. Kapitel 43–55,* vol. 5/3 of *Gesamtausgabe* (Frankfurt am Main: Suhrkamp, 1977), 1628. Translated by Neville Plaice et al., under the title *Principle of Hope,* vol. 3 (Cambridge, MA: MIT Press, 1986), 1375-76.

and Marx. If we have no great hopes of the justification that might be expected from human activity alone, then we must face the question whether we are not *condemned* through our planned action to bring universal peace by means of a "world domestic politics." Can humanity survive except by an extreme and ultimate moral effort?[27] An enormous burden is then laid upon us. This is the law under which we live. This law forces us to be the Atlas, who, like the figure in the Greek myth, bears the whole weight of the world on his shoulders. Jean-Paul Sartre says, "we are condemned to be free."[28] In this freedom to which we are condemned we have to be like Atlas. We cannot remove the burden. Must we not break under it? Can we gain any distance at all from our actions under it? Or are we always ruthlessly riveted to our own works and their consequences? Friedrich Hölderlin lamented this question in his poem, "Der Archipelagus":

> Alas, our race wanders by night, it dwells as in Orkus
> without the divine. They are chained
> to their own efforts, in the roaring workplace
> each hears only himself; the wild ones must work
> with their powerful arms, restless,
> but like the furies, the labors of the poor remain fruitless.[29]

---

27. Cf. Carl Friedrich von Weizsäcker, *Bedingungen des Friedens,* 6th ed. (Göttingen: Vandenhoeck & Ruprecht, 1964), 18. However, he argues as well that "the way is at its best prepared by the political order and moral conduct, but it leads through suffering and grace." Cf. Carl Friedrich von Weizsäcker, *Die Zeit drängt — Das Ende der Geduld. Aufruf und Diskussion* (Munich: Deutscher Taschenbuch-Verlag, 1989), 45.

28. Jean-Paul Sartre, "L'Existentialisme est un Humanisme" (Paris: Nagel, 1970), 7-36, esp. 16. Translated by Philip Mairet under the title *Existentialism and Humanism* (London: Eyre Meuthen & Co., Ltd., 1973).

29. Friedrich Hölderlin, *Der Archipelagus,* vol. 5 of the Tiessen Edition, ed. Paul Eliasberg (New-Isenburg: Tiessen, 1978). Translated under the title *The Archipelago: The Text* (London: Critic Press, 1940).

Chapter Three

The Passive Righteousness of Faith

Death of the Old Adam; Life of the New Human

As a result of the "journey around the world," the experience of human cultural achievement, Kleist has no firm hope but can only cautiously conjecture that "perhaps the back door to paradise is open." Martin Luther, on the contrary, tells of a return to paradise that has already happened: "I felt then that I had been born anew and had entered paradise itself through opened gates."[1] This new birth and second naïveté were not the outcome of a gracefulness and charm achieved by us. Grace can only be freely granted. It is experienced only as a gift. This justification and righteousness which cannot be attained and won by us is the righteousness of faith. It is neither a justifying thinking nor justifying acting, neither contemplative nor active righteousness. It is a passive righteousness.

The righteousness of faith is passive[2] in the sense "that we let God alone work in us and that in all our powers we do nothing of our own."[3]

---

1. Luther, *Vorrede zum ersten Band seiner lateinischen Schriften* (1545), WA 54:186,8f.; LW 34:337; *Luthers Werke in Auswahl,* 8 volumes, ed. A. Leitzmann and O. Clemen (Berlin: de Gruyter, 1962-1967), 4:428,1f. [hereafter cited as Cl]; *Martin Luther. Ausgewählte Schriften,* ed. K. Bornkamm and Gerhard Ebeling (Frankfurt: Insel-Verlag, 1982), I:23 [hereafter cited as IL]. Cf. the texts in the Appendix.

2. Cf. WA 40/I,45, 24-26ff.; LW 26:7-8 and WA 54:186,7; LW 34:337.

3. Luther, "Von den guten Werken" (1520), WA 6:244,3-6; LW 44:72; Cl 1:267,31-34; IL I:101. That God alone works in us without using any power of ours, cf. "Dies sind die

"Faith, however, is a divine work within us which changes us and makes us to be born anew of God, John 1[:12-13]. It kills the old Adam and makes us altogether different men, in heart, spirit and mind and powers."[4] Faith is wholly and entirely God's work. It is not our own decision, interpretive activity, or construction of meaning.[5] This is the first and most important thing that we have to say about faith. In its significance for people of modernity we cannot rate it too highly. In this regard the Enlightenment is opposed to the Reformation. Reaching a climax in the philosophy of Immanuel Kant, the Enlightenment claimed that with the faculties of pure recollection and pure construction it could evaluate even the faith. Or there is at least the claim to discover faith in the self, for example as the feeling of absolute dependence. We humans want to make things by ourselves, including faith, or at least we want to assure ourselves of faith. For Luther, however, faith is solely the work of God. Faith encounters us by coming to us.[6] We experience it in that we suffer it.

The experience of faith is painful. When Luther spoke about the death of the old Adam, this was no mere metaphor.

> He who has not been brought low, reduced to nothing through the cross and suffering, takes credit for works and wisdom and does not give credit to God. . . . He, however, who has emptied himself [cf. Phil. 2:7] through suffering no longer does works but knows that God works and does all things in him. . . . It is this that Christ says in John 3[:7], "You must be born anew." To be born anew, one must consequently first die.[7]

---

heil'gen zehn Gebot" in *Evangelisches Gesangbuch* (Stuttgart: Gesangbuchverlag, 1996), #231,4 [hereafter cited as EG]: "Leave off your own work so that God may work in you."

4. Luther, "Vorrede auf die Epistel S. Pauli an die Römer" (1522), in *Luthers Vorreden zur Bible,* 3rd ed., edited by Heinrich Bornkamm (Göttingen: Vandenhoeck & Ruprecht, 1989 [originally Vandenhoeck Kleine Reihe no. 1550]), 182; WADB 7:10,6-8; LW 35:370; cf. Deut. 6:5.

5. Cf. WA 12:484,17–485,2.

6. Gal. 3:23 and 25, "Now before faith came, we were imprisoned and guarded under the law until faith would be revealed. . . . But now that faith has come, we are no longer subject to a disciplinarian [. . .]."

7. Luther, "Heidelberg Disputation" (1518), WA 1:363,33-36; LW 31:55; Cl 5:390,17-20.

The passive righteousness of faith takes place when justifying thinking (metaphysics) and justifying doing (morality), together with the unity of both that some seek, are all radically destroyed. In other words, both metaphysics and morality with their claim to justify our being are brought to nothing by the work of God. God slays, but he does so only to make alive. "The Lord kills and brings to life; he brings down to Sheol and raises up."[8]

We now need to grasp more closely what the death of the old Adam, the "descent into the hell of self-knowledge,"[9] involves. We then need to ask about the constitution of the life that is given anew. We will once again differentiate thinking from action, metaphysics from morality. Looking at the two components of faith, death on the one side, life on the other, we will first consider the angle of action.

Doing — Morality — Praxis

The need that lies deeply within each of us to prove our right to exist — not simply to be there, but to gain recognition by what we can afford and accomplish — is put to death. This will to achieve and thus to secure recognition by being active and productive has become part of our nature, our second and evil nature. This nature "is very unwilling to die and to suffer, and it is a bitter holy day for nature to cease from its own work and be dead."[10]

The reverse side of this death of the old Adam is a supreme springing to life. This is no paradox. When I am nailed down to what I have done and do, and let myself be nailed down by others, I am then profoundly not free. But when I am freed from this lack of freedom, then distance and sense of proportion come with the freedom I am granted, and thus comes the room that is needed for action. Luther can thus extol the supreme vitality that faith brings, the work of God within that slays the

---

8. 1 Sam. 2:6.

9. Johann G. Hamann, *Sämtliche Werke*, vol. 2, 164, 18. Cf. Kant, *Die Metaphysik der Sitten, Tugendlehre* (1797), vol. 7 of *Werke in zehn Bänden*, § 14, 576. Translated and edited by Mary Gregor under the title *Groundwork of the Metaphysics of Morals* (Cambridge, UK, and New York: Cambridge University Press, 1997), 191.

10. WA 6:244,3-6 and 248, 26f; LW 44:78; Cl 1:271,40–272,1; IL 1:108.

old Adam: "What a vital, busy, active, and mighty thing is faith, the faith that makes it impossible not to be always doing good works. It never asks whether good works are to be done, but before one asks it has done and still does them."[11] The righteousness of faith that God effects and we can only suffer is a supremely active thing, precisely because of the suffering experience of the divine work. This righteousness is never without works. "Therefore I wish to have the words 'without works' understood in the following manner: Not that the righteous person does nothing, but that his works do not make him righteous, rather that his [granted] righteousness creates works."[12]

Thinking — Metaphysics — Theory

What must be said about the action of the passively justified has also to be said about their thinking, their theoretical perception of God, the world, and themselves. The justifying thinking that tries to settle the conflict of justifications and to fashion a concept of the "unity" of reality is put to death. This metaphysical approach and conclusion is in league with justifying action and morality. Justifying thinking seeks to mediate and reconcile all things. Its driving compulsion is to prove that everything individual and particular has the general as its basis. This is how it links up with justifying action. In so doing, it becomes ideological, blind to reality. It "calls evil good and good evil." It misunderstands and perverts the truth of things and relations.

The ideological thinking of justifying metaphysics, allied as it is to morality as justifying action, is put to death in the passive righteousness of faith. Those who through suffering and the cross are born anew as Christians and theologians, the "theologians of the cross," call things by their right names. "A theology of glory calls evil good and good evil. A theology of the cross calls the thing what it actually is."[13] A theologian of

11. *Luthers Vorreden zur Bibel,* 182; WADB 7:10,9-12; LW 35:370.
12. WA 1:364,6-8; LW 31:55-56; Cl 5:390,27-30.
13. WA 1:354,21f.; LW 31:40; Cl 5:379,5f.

the cross perceives and says what the real issue is, for the view of God which one seeks with one's own powers, in which everything would be rounded off under the concept of the one, the true, and the good, has now been shattered in a painful disillusionment. The death of the old nature lies last but not least in the fact that the illusion of a totality of meaning, even if only hypothetical and anticipatory, has been overthrown. Theologians of the cross find in the deeply seated need for justifying thinking the radically evil "imaginations and thoughts of the human heart."[14] The human heart as *cor fingens*,[15] a fabricating heart, constantly produces and projects in its justifying thinking images of meaning: idols to which the heart attaches itself, stars, models, the goals of good fortune and success. We all have aims of this kind. Our heart attaches itself to them after having fabricated them. That is why Calvin, in accordance with Luther, described the human heart as "a perpetual factory of idols," a *fabrica idolorum*.[16] Concepts of metaphysics can also become idolatrous. Even the teaching of the church and theology can produce idolatrous images out of the divine attributes if we ignore the cross of Christ when speaking about such attributes as power, wisdom, goodness, and righteousness. In Luther's exposition of the twentieth thesis of the 1518 *Heidelberg Disputation* we read that "none of us can talk adequately or profitably about God's glory and majesty unless we see God also in the lowliness and humiliation of the cross."[17] Christian theology does not begin in the heights as other religions do; it begins in the depths,[18] in the womb of Mary and the death of Jesus on the cross. "The glory of our God is precisely that for our sakes he comes down to the very depths, into human flesh, into the

---

14. Cf. Gen. 6:5, 8:21.

15. WA 42:348,37f.; LW 2:117-18. Luther uses Genesis 8:21 as a defining text, which indicates that the human is a rational being with a heart which forms images *(animal rationale, habens cor fingens)*. Cf. Oswald Bayer, "Rationalitat und Utopie" in *Umstrittene Freiheit. Theologisch-philosophische Kontroversen,* Uni-Taschenbücher, no. 1092 (Tübingen: J. C. B. Mohr [Paul Siebeck], 1981), 135-51.

16. John Calvin, *Institutes of the Christian Religion,* trans. Ford Lewis Battles, ed. John T. McNeill, vol. XX of *The Library of Christian Classics* (Philadelphia: Westminster, 1960), I,11,8, p. 108.

17. WA 1:362,11-13; LW 33:52; Cl 5:388,22-24.

18. WA 10,I/2.297,9f.

bread, into our mouth, our heart, our bosom."[19] "Philosophy and the worldly wise are unwilling to begin here and therefore they are fools. We have to begin in the depths and rise up from them."[20]

On the other hand, we must not make the cross into a principle, as has happened even within the thinking of theology and the preaching of the church from the time of Hegel's philosophy. It is still the danger of our age to turn the cross of Jesus Christ into a principle evident to everyone, so that a "natural" theology of the cross emerges. The task in church proclamation and theological reflection is to steer between the Scylla of a natural theology of glory, unmasked by Luther in the *Heidelberg Disputation,* and the presently much closer Charybdis of a natural theology of the cross. A natural theology of glory and a natural theology of the cross are both forms of natural theology, and they are both perversions of the passive righteousness of faith.

The heart, profoundly evil in its distortion, composes with both religious fantasy and metaphysical concepts "a human notion that some people call faith;"[21] it speculates. The illusion that arises out of the need for religious and metaphysical justification is so strong that not even the gospel is safe against it. This is as true today as it was in Luther's time. "By their own powers [they] create an idea in their heart which says, 'I believe'; they take this then to be a true faith. But [. . .] it is a human figment and idea that never reaches the depths of the heart." It is an act of consciousness that never reaches into the depths of human existence to save. "Nothing comes of it . . . and no improvement follows."[22]

Neither Theory nor Praxis

Luther was perspicacious enough to see that the gospel will not let itself be pressed into a schema of theory and praxis. He perceived that those for whom the gospel is a theory, "a human figment and idea," are forced to

19. WA 23:157,30-32; LW 37:72.
20. WA 10,I/2:297,7-10.
21. *Luthers Vorreden zur Bibel,* 182; WADB 7:8,30f.; LW 35:370. Cf. WA 12:483,8–484,2.
22. *Luthers Vorreden zur Bibel,* 182; WADB 7:10,1-5; LW 35:370.

demand that it also be fulfilled in praxis. With the schema of theory and praxis "they fall into the error of saying, 'Faith is not enough; one must do works.'"[23] In other words, they think that sanctification must be added to justification.

Faith is neither a theory nor a praxis of self-fulfillment. It is a passive righteousness, namely, the work of God in us that we experience with suffering, dying both to justifying thinking and justifying action. The meaning is not that faith is both unthinking and inactive. By it, rather, both thinking and action are renewed.

The Gift of Self-Forgetfulness

Those who are born anew are no longer entangled with themselves. They are solidly freed from this entanglement, from the self-reflection that always seeks what belongs to itself. This is not a deadening of self. It does not flee from thought and responsibility. No, it is the gift of self-forgetfulness. The passive righteousness of faith tells us: You do not concern yourself at all! In that God does what is decisive in us, we may live outside ourselves and solely in him. Thus, we are hidden from ourselves, and removed from the judgment of others or the judgment of ourselves about ourselves as a final judgment. "Who am I?" Such self-reflection never finds peace in itself. Resolution comes only in the prayer to which Bonhoeffer[24] surrendered it and in which he was content to leave it. "Who am I? Thou knowest me. I am thine, O God!"[25]

This new way of existing cannot secure itself, just as it is the liberation from all efforts at self-stabilization and self-organization. Even physically we cannot for a single moment with our own resources continue to exist and not perish.[26] We could not live if breath was not constantly given

23. *Luthers Vorreden zur Bibel,* 182; WADB 7:8,32-34; LW 35:370.

24. See note 2 in Chapter 1.

25. In *Act and Being* Bonhoeffer quotes Luther: "Seek yourself only in Christ and not in yourself, and you will find yourself in him eternally." *Dietrich Bonhoeffer Works,* vol. 2, ed. Wayne Whitson Floyd, Jr., trans. H. Martin Rumscheidt from the German edition by Hans-Richard Reuter (Minneapolis: Fortress, 1996). See also WA 2:690,24f.; LW 42:106.

26. Luther, *The Bondage of the Will* (1525), WA 18:662,12; LW 33:103; Cl 3:151,27.

to us and never withheld for a moment. Similarly, our new way of existing has its reality only in the breathing of prayer. "Pray God that he may work faith in you. Otherwise you will surely remain forever without faith, regardless of what you may think or do."[27] The Lutheran Tobias Clausnitzer (1618-1684) has left us a prayer of this kind that is now a hymn:

> All our knowledge, sense, and sight
> Lie in deepest darkness shrouded
> Till your Spirit breaks the night,
> Filling us with light unclouded.
> All good thoughts and all good living
> Come but by your gracious giving.[28]

The desire to seek self-assurance and to find one's identity can lead only into the darkness of uncertainty. Faith, however, involves liberation from the drive for self-assurance and therefore from uncertainty. It means liberation from the search for identity and its attempted discovery. In prayer I am led away from myself. I am torn away from self and set outside the self with its abilities and judgments. I may look away from myself. "Pay no regard to what you yourself are."[29] At this basic and decisive point and place, here where my existence is grounded, I may look away from myself and have absolutely nothing to do with self. "For faith is a living, daring confidence in God's grace, so sure and certain that the believer would stake his life on it a thousand times." It is "more sure and certain than all experience and life itself."[30]

---

27. *Luthers Vorreden zur Bibel,* 183; WADB 7:10,25-27; LW 35:371.

28. "Liebster Jesu, wir sind hier," EG, #162, v. 2. Translated and adapted by Catherine Winkworth under the title "Dearest Jesus, at your Word," *Lutheran Book of Worship* (Minneapolis: Augsburg Publishing House, et al., 1978), #248, v. 2 [hereafter cited as LBW].

29. Jochen Klepper, *Kyrie: Geistliche Lieder,* 17th ed. (Bielefeld: Luther-Verlag, 1980), 29ff. Klepper cites Luther's 1528 Christmas sermon: "Noli respicere, quod tu es, sed eum qui ad te venit. . . . You must not look at what you are, but at what happens to you here and now." WA 27:492,5f., 16f. Cf. Klepper, *Unter dem Schatten deiner Flügel. Aus den Tagebüchern der Jahre 1932-1942,* ed. H. Klepper (Stuttgart: Deutsche Verlags-Anstalt, 1956), 531, cf. p. 322. Cf. WATR 6:303,8f. (no. 6979): "Lift up your eyes at once and see the man who is called Christ."

30. *Luthers Vorreden zur Bibel,* 183; WADB 7:10,16f.; LW 35:370-71 and *The Bondage of the Will,* WA 18:605,33f.; LW 33:24; Cl 3:100,33.

Faith is a venture. Yet we do not venture into the void — "take a chance and see what you get."[31] We should not compare it with throwing a stone at random. As confidence in the grace of God, faith is a well-founded risk. How we encounter grace as our basis of confidence and the manner in which it communicates itself to us in the word of promise, will be our theme in the following. Our concern now is to emphasize the new relation to the world that is given and opened up in faith. "This knowledge of and confidence in God's grace makes men glad and bold and happy in dealing with God and with all other creatures. And this is the work which the Holy Spirit performs in faith."[32]

This boldness is not at all subjective, but rather it is something upon which we can rely and depend. It is already there at hand, so that we can hold onto it. The boldness of faith lies in the word that is given to it. That is why Luther can say that the sure and certain confidence and knowledge of divine grace can make us joyful and bold, taking pleasure in God and all other creatures.

Renaissance: New Relation to the World

The new human is no grotesque caricature who spends his life in a darkened room, reciting with closed eyes, "I am justified by faith alone, I am justified by faith alone."[33] By contrast, the passive righteousness of faith with its new relation to God and the self creates a new relation to all creatures, to the world, including a new perception of time and space.

It is important that we especially emphasize this point, for an ancient and stubborn prejudice, of which the proclamation of the church and the thinking of theology are not innocent, has prevented us from perceiving the new relation to the world that is included in the righteousness

31. WA 4:624,21. See also Oswald Bayer, *Promissio. Geschichte der reformatorischen Wende in Luthers Theologie* (Göttingen: Vandenhoeck & Ruprecht, 1971), 324; WA 19:224,26-28 on Jonah 2:3: "Even though they cry and pray to the winds, may it hit the mark or not, it is nothing and it achieves nothing."

32. *Luthers Vorreden zur Bibel,* 183; WADB 7:10,17-19; LW 35:370-71.

33. On this vision of Swedenborg, see Erik Peterson, "Kierkegaard und der Protestantismus," *Marginalien zur Theologie* (Munich: Kösel, 1956), 26.

of faith and opened up by it. According to the dominant opinion, the righteousness of faith not only focuses upon the point of the relationship with God but is even limited to it. In its denial of all relationships to the world and isolation from them, it is construed to be unworldly. This prejudice flourishes because we usually entangle ourselves in the alternative of secularization or desecularization, of optimism or pessimism. For this reason, we completely fail to understand the distinctive courage of life, beyond these alternatives and overcoming them, that we ought to learn from Luther.

"I felt then that I had been born anew and had entered paradise itself through opened gates." This witness of Luther regarding his receiving of the passive righteousness of faith as the gift and work of God in the total context of all that he said from the pulpit, on the rostrum, and at table, is to be understood cosmologically. By the word "cosmological" we do not mean something that is isolated from theological perception. For we cannot conceive of a view of the world that lies outside theology and the justification dispute. Outside theology, outside belief and unbelief, outside the Word that creates faith, there is no world.

We do not leave the world when we return to paradise and are born anew and created afresh. We are still in the world, and we enter into a new worldliness. The "new creation" is a return to the world, not a retreat from it. The new creation is a conversion to the world, as a conversion to the Creator, hearing God's voice speaking to us and addressing us through his creatures. Augustine was wrong to say that his voice draws us away from God's creatures into the inner self and then to transcendence.[34] Counteracting Augustine's inwardness in its withdrawal from the world, Luther emphasizes the penetrating this-worldliness of God. God wills to be the Creator by speaking to us only through his creatures.[35]

---

34. Cf., for example, Augustine, *Confessions,* X, 6, 8.

35. The sense in which Luther speaks of God's address "through" the creature may be seen from his sermon on Mark 7:31-37 (September 8, 1538), WA 46:493-95. For an analysis of this, cf. Oswald Bayer, "Tu dich auf! Verbum sanans et salvificans und das Problem der 'natürlichen' Theologie," *Schöpfung als Anrede. Zu einer Hermeneutik der Schöpfung,* 2nd ed. (Tübingen: Mohr Siebeck, 1990), 62-79.

"In the Dawn of the Life to Come"

Faith as "a living and daring reliance upon the grace of God" in its relation to the creatures of God is impressively expounded in the following *Table Talk*. We are now, Luther said,

> in the dawn of the life to come, for we have begun to recapture our knowledge of the creatures that we lost with Adam's fall. We can see the creatures properly now, more than was ever possible under the papacy. Erasmus had little interest here. He never investigated how the fruit is formed and prepared and made in the mother's womb, and hence had little regard for the glorious estate of marriage. Beginning with the grace of God, however, we can know God's wonderful works and miracles even from the little flowers, when we consider the divine omnipotence and the divine goodness. We thus laud and praise and thank God. For we see in his creatures the power of his Word, how mighty it is. He spoke and it came to be [Ps. 33:9] — even in a peach stone, for in due time the very hard shell will open up for the soft core that is within. Erasmus completely misses such things. He does not consider them. He sees the creatures as a cow sees a new barn door.[36]

The first sentence of this *Table Talk* discourse, which is a summary of the whole, shows us that Luther has no nature idyll in view. Neither do we find here the high-minded consciousness of the "renaissance man," that he belonged to a newly dawning age, one that he would himself bring in with his own reason and resources. The "dawn of the life to come" depends instead upon "the grace of God," and "now" is when the grace of God makes itself heard anew.[37] Now it opens ears and eyes and hearts and mouths and hands to look upon the world as a creation. "We have begun to recapture our knowledge of the creatures that we lost with Adam's fall."

Like all Luther's theology, this *Table Talk* discourse is defined by the interweaving of times, enunciated by Paul in Romans 8:18-23, that elimi-

---

36. WATR 1:574,8-19 (no. 1160).
37. See 2 Cor. 6:2, "See, now is the acceptable time; see, now is the day of salvation!"

nates the alternative of either a backward look at creation or else a forward look at consummation. Those who are painfully aware of the contradiction between the suffering and sighing creatures of the present world and the promised creation of the original world will never close their eyes upon the world but will always keep them open so that they may see the newly manifested glory of creation. They are astonished.

This astonishment differs from the unbroken devotion to the cosmos that many people now feel to be a means of salvation in the ecological crisis, and that many others are at least seeking. If this astonishment, as testified in the *Table Talk* discourse, requires nothing less than a rebirth as an antidote to Adam's fall and loss, if it is a renaissance that God himself effects, then it is no naïve astonishment. It involves no aesthetically immediate relationship with nature. Instead, it arises out of the overcoming of a deep rupture, out of the victory over death and the powers of death.

In the Belly of the Fish

The new relationship to the world comes about only through death. The new astonishment, the second naïveté, arises out of the overcoming of the world of death in which we have let ourselves be entrapped and into which our fellow creatures are entrapped through our own faults. We have not done justice to them. With our need for justification we entangle ourselves in the web of guilt to which Paul refers in Romans 8:18-23, and Anaximander in his own way before him. Luther says that we experience the world either in sin and unbelief or else in faith: faith *in* the grace of God and faith *as* the grace of God. In unbelief we experience the world as the wrath of God. Luther knows no neutral zone on the far side of grace and wrath. Into the new world come those who know the grace of God in faith, faith as a living and daring reliance upon grace, so that in the presence of God they can confess as in Psalm 31:8: "You have set my feet in a spacious place."[38] This new world is closed, however, to those who have not previously been in the narrow belly of the fish and known the dread of

38. Cf. Ps. 118:5.

the prophet Jonah, of which we are guilty ourselves. The sea and water and everything created "make the world too narrow for us and make us conscious of a wrathful God. Many who are suffering great distress say: 'It seems to me that heaven and earth are lying upon me.'"[39] Clearly, then, what Luther said about the recapturing of a knowledge of the creature that was lost with Adam's fall, about the dawn of the life to come, was no idyll and involved no immediate spirituality of the cosmos. It was instead a second naïveté following the harsh rupture and death itself.

In order to intensify the issue, we must look further at Luther's exposition of Jonah 2:3: "You cast me into the deep, into the heart of the seas, and the flood surrounded me; all your waves and your billows passed over me."

> In this passage we can see the state of Jonah's heart before he cries to God. He forgets those who had thrust him into the sea. He says that God had done it. "Thou," he says, "thou didst cast me into the deep." For he felt in his conscience that all the misfortune that overtakes us is the wrath of God. And all the creatures think they see here only God and his wrath even in a driven leaf, as we read in Leviticus 26:36: "The sound of a driven leaf shall frighten them!" Is not this a great marvel? Nothing is smaller or arouses more scorn than a dry leaf lying on the earth. All the little worms run over it. It cannot defend itself even against bits of dust. When Job wanted to rate his own insignificance, he could think of nothing with which to compare himself in God's presence but a dry leaf. Nevertheless, when the hour comes, the right moment, the sound of this leaf will frighten horse and rider and spear and armor and king and prince and all the host and its might who would not otherwise be scared by hell itself. The rustling of such a leaf will make the world too narrow for us. It will be for us the wrathful God whom we have previously crushed and defied in the face of heaven and earth. But if a driven leaf can do this, what will the deep sea do of which Jonah speaks? He does not say: "The waves and billows passed over me," but "your waves and your billows passed over me," because he feels in his conscience that the sea and its

39. WA 19:226,27f. and 227,8f.

waves and billows are the servants of God and his wrath and their punishment of sin.[40]

This sin is that of an unbelieving flight from God.

A Spacious Place

"Just as distress is a narrow place, which casts us down and cramps us, so God's help is our large place which makes us free and happy."[41]

Mortal trouble, anxiety, and narrowness lie on the one side, breadth and breath and liberation on the other. This finds expression in the distinction and interrelationship of lament and answering, lamenting at death and praise for deliverance from death. We find therein the way in which Luther felt about the world, his distinctive experience of time and space. It may be seen most forcefully in his exposition of Psalm 90: "In the midst of earthly life, snares of death surround us." Luther agrees with the beginning of this ancient antiphon, but the cross of Jesus Christ leads him to reverse it: "In the midst of certain death, life in Christ is ours."[42] Time and space are experienced as narrowness or breadth, as death or life, as wrath or grace, as affliction or liberation. Nature and history never fall apart for Luther as they do for us. The two both tell us "nothing else than God's work, that is grace and wrath."[43] And we ourselves are creatures with whom "God speaks in an eternal and immortal way, whether in anger or in grace,"[44] for with all other creatures we are addressed in a way that can never be revoked.

40. WA 19:226,9–227,4; cf. 225,28f., "Each of us has his own hell with him wherever we are so long as we feel the ultimate miseries of death and the wrath of God."

41. WA 31/I:93,27-29 on Psalm 118; LW 14:59. The German "weiter Raum" can be translated more aptly as "spacious place."

42. WA 40/III:484-594 (1534/35), esp. 495,3f.; LW 13:83 (n. 16); EG, #518; LBW #350 (in part). These two phrases are Luther's reversal of lines in the famous medieval hymn, "Media vita in morte sumus," which he had published in German translation in 1525 (cf. WA 35:126-32, 453, 454).

43. Luther, "Historia Galeatii Capellae," (1538) preface, WA 50:385,15f.; LW 34:277; IL V:179.

44. WA 43:481,32-35; LW 5:76. Cf. Preface to the Sermons on Genesis (1527), WA 24:22,31–23,32.

Faith orients itself to the ultimate goal, the resurrection of the dead and eternal life, and in so doing it relies only upon the one who justifies the ungodly. First and last it is "a living, daring confidence in God's grace, so sure and certain that the believer would stake his life on it." It is a "divine work in us which changes us and makes us to be born anew of God."[45]

These short statements from the preface to Romans are expounded here in relation to eschatology, i.e., to the end of the world reaching its consummation through judgment, by reference to the third section of Luther's 1519 sermon, *On Preparation for Death*. This is an unusually impressive section; those who hear it will never forget it. Luther deals here with the apocalyptic and New Testament imagery of the birth pangs of the end time. He radicalizes the imagery in such a way as to see the process of birth from the perspective, not of the mother, but of the infant, that is itself passive during the birth. This reversal of perspective offers a fine illustration of the linguistically creative way in which the passive righteousness of faith works. We get a full sense here of the great importance that the experience of the passive righteousness of faith had for Luther, and this will help us to understand fully what it means to live by faith.

> In preparing to die, we should turn our eyes to God, to whom the path of death leads and directs us. Here we find the beginning of the narrow gate and of the straight path to life [Matt. 7:17]. All must venture forth on this path, for though the gate is quite narrow, the path is not long. Just as an infant is born with peril and pain from the small abode of its mother's womb into this immense heaven and earth, that is, into this world, so man departs this life through the narrow gate of death. And although the heaven and the earth in which we dwell at present seem large and wide to us, they are nevertheless as narrow and small in comparison with the future heaven as the mother's womb is in comparison with this our heaven [i.e., sky]. Therefore, the death of the dear saints is called a new birth, and their feast day is known in Latin as *natale,* that is, the day of their birth. However, the

---

45. *Luthers Vorreden zur Bibel,* 182f.; WADB 7:10,16f.; 6f.; LW 35:370.

narrow passage of death makes us think of this life as expansive and
the life beyond as confined. Therefore, we must believe this and learn
a lesson from the physical birth of a child, as Christ declares, "When a
woman is in travail she has sorrow; but when she has recovered, she
no longer remembers the anguish, since a child is born by her into the
world" [John 16:21]. So it is that in dying we must bear this anguish
and know that a large mansion and joy will follow [John 14:2].[46]

Such daring hope is hope for the resurrection of the dead, hope for
liberation from the jaws of anguish into a spacious place where there is no
affliction.[47] This comes only by way of the passive righteousness of faith,
in which God justifies the ungodly,[48] just as creation out of nothing can
be known only from this experience. A comparison of Romans 4:17 and
Romans 4:5 will make this clear. The justification of the ungodly —
death of the old and birth of the new human — this "divine work in us" is
nothing else but the work of him who created new things out of nothing,
giving life to the dead and existence to the nonexistent.[49] Luther, then,
confesses both creation out of nothing and the resurrection of the dead
when he tells of his reformation discovery of the passive righteousness of
faith, saying: "I felt then that I had been born anew and had entered paradise itself through opened gates."

Faith and Action: The New Obedience

Faith is assured of perfect joy in the spacious place of freedom, not because this joy is already visible, but because this joy has been promised.
I have heard of it but as yet have seen nothing of it. "Not in essence, but

46. WA 2:685,20–686,8; LW 42:99-100 (translation slightly altered); IL II:16f. Cf.
WATR 3:276,26f. (no. 3339).
47. See Job 36:16, "He also allured you out of distress into a broad place where there
was no constraint."
48. See Rom. 4:5, "But to one who without works trusts him who justifies the ungodly, such faith is reckoned righteousness."
49. See Rom. 4:17, "in the presence of the God in whom he believed, who gives life to
the dead and calls into existence the things that do not exist."

by promise, I have eternal life. I have it in obscurity. I do not see it, but I believe it and will hereafter surely feel it."[50]

In our time and space, with all its hopelessness and obscurities, we do not live by sight. Here and now it is only the old Adam with his justifying thinking that attempts a comprehensive theory of world history. The old Adam within us wants to find meaning; he is concerned to assure himself about the meaning of the whole. Faith frees us from this concern. It enables us to accept the finitude of our lives and of the many histories into which they are interwoven in the battle for justification, the life-and-death struggle for recognition. We can accept our finitude, yet still with sorrow and melancholy, lamenting our transitoriness.

Not Condemned to Success

My life history, together with all others, is justified by God, by grace alone, *gratis,* for nothing. Therefore Ecclesiastes says, according to Luther, that everything we do is for nothing, "vanity" and futility. What does this "for nothing" of futility have to do with the "for nothing" of grace? How does it relate to the fact that our justification takes place "for nothing" and rests neither on justifying action nor justifying thinking, the understandable metaphysical need to give life meaning? Following Luther's preface to Ecclesiastes,

> the title of this book ought to show that it is written against free will, for it points out that all that we advise and propose and execute is for nothing and futile. It always turns out differently from what we think and desire. He teaches us in this way to relax and leave things only to God, without or in opposition to our knowledge and advice. We must not think that the book is scolding the creatures of God when it says that everything is vanity and wretchedness. . . . For God's creatures are all good [Gen. 1:31 and 1 Tim. 4:4]. He also teaches us that one should have a good heart with one's wife and make good use of life.[51]

50. WA 16:52,19-21.
51. Luther, Preface to Ecclesiastes (1524), in *Luthers Vorreden zur Bibel,* 80f.; WADB 10/II:104,26–106,6. Cf. WA 20:7,5f., 29-32.

35

"Go, eat your bread with enjoyment, and drink your wine with a merry heart. . . . Enjoy life with the wife whom you love. . . . Whatever your hand finds to do, do with your might."[52]

Finite joys have their place and validity and beauty. Enjoing what is finite means to use it in a way justified by God. The skepticism of Ecclesiastes does not refer to this. Vanity applies only to our yearnings for immortality, the infinite attempts to ensure and establish the finite, to the achieving of fulfillment by endless progress. The skepticism sees to it that our claims to totality are sobered down. It tells us

> that what we propose and do in dealing with creatures will be done in vain and uselessly unless we are content to do what is immediately to hand and not to seek to master and control the future. So we constantly retrogress, so that we have nothing but lost toil and trouble. What occurs is what God wills and thinks, not what we want. What Christ says in Matthew 6:34, "So do not worry about tomorrow, for tomorrow will bring worries of its own. Today's trouble is enough for today," expounds on Ecclesiastes and brings out its content. God is the one who takes care of us. Our worrying is useless and causes us much trouble.[53]

A distinctive understanding of time, a peculiar perception of the time of our own lives and of all history! What is the point of acting and planning in such a finite span of time? Is it not condemned to futility? Is it not arbitrary when human action does not fit into a perceptible cosmic and historical context, let alone establish such a context? Is it not arbitrary when we have to be skeptical in relation to both a contemplative and an active theodicy? Does it make no difference what we do?

What does it mean, however, when Luther says with Ecclesiastes 9:10 that one should be of a merry heart, and do what lies at hand: "whatever your hand finds to do, do with your might"? (Luther more frequently quotes 1 Samuel 10:7 in this connection.) Do not think that you first have to look at the total plan and progress of the world, if you are to know what actions will now make sense, and where they will lead!

52. Eccles. 9:7-10.
53. *Luthers Vorreden zur Bibel;* WADB 10/II:106,6-15.

"Doing Whatever Your Hand Finds to Do"

In the new obedience Luther takes a sober view of the sphere in which we are set, the sphere of *worldly* righteousness that is not burdened with concern for salvation. In this sphere, we ourselves must do all that we have to do "as if there were no God." This astonishing statement occurs in his 1524 exposition of Psalm 127,[54] in which he depicts his basic understanding of the rule of God in state and household, in the political and economic realms. The Psalm itself reflects upon the relation of divine and human work, of divine and human concerns: "Unless the Lord builds the house, those who build it labor in vain. Unless the Lord guards the city, the guard keeps watch in vain. It is in vain that you rise up early and go late to rest, eating the bread of anxious toil; for he provides for his beloved during sleep."[55] If we can understand this, then we understand what it means to live by faith.

What are the consequences for responsible human action for our caring and planning?

> Are we to provide no supplies, leave our gates and windows open, make no effort to defend ourselves but allow ourselves to be pierced through like lifeless corpses . . . ? By no means. You have just heard that those in authority should be watchful and diligent, and perform all the duties of their office: bar the gates, defend the towers and walls, put on armor, and procure supplies. In general, they should proceed as if there were no God and they had to rescue themselves and manage their own affairs; just as the head of a household is supposed to work as if he were trying to sustain himself by his own labors.
>
> But he must watch out that his heart never comes to rely on these deeds of his, and get arrogant when things go well or worried when

54. WA 15:348-79; LW 45:317-37. Cf. the 1532/33 exposition in WA 40/III:202-69. Cf. also WA 30/III:277,34, 278,9f.; LW 47:13: "As if there were no God." Luther emphasizes the hypothetical character of this phrase, saying, "we are now speaking as in a dream."

55. Ps. 127:1-2. The NRSV provides this alternative translation in a footnote: "for he provides for his beloved during sleep." This corresponds to Luther's own German translation: "denn seinen Freunden gibt er es im Schlaf." See *Die Bibel nach der Übersetzung Martin Luthers* (Stuttgart: Deutsche Bibelgesellschaft, 1985).

things go wrong. He should regard all such preparation and equipment as being the work of our Lord God under a mask, as it were, beneath which he himself alone effects and accomplishes what we desire. He commands us so to equip ourselves for this reason also, that he might conceal his own work under this disguise, and allow those who boast to go their way [run against a wall], and strengthen those who are worried, so that men will not tempt him . . . in like manner, through their own labor he made Abraham, Isaac, and Jacob wealthy, etc. Indeed, one could very well say that the course of the world, and especially the doing of his saints, are God's mask, under which he conceals himself and so marvelously exercises dominion and rustles about in the world.[56]

The course of this world and that of their own lives are so concealed even from those who are justified by faith that they cannot conceive or experience the divine and the human concern for the world as a harmonious relationship. This ambiguity extends even to the works of the justified done in the new obedience. But this does not mean that they are arbitrary. The fact that we cannot penetrate the web of motives behind our actions, and fail to foresee, let alone to predetermine, their results, should not prevent the concern and the basic needs of our neighbors and all our fellow creatures from showing us plainly enough what we ought to do. "Whatever your hand finds to do, do it with your might!" Those whom God justifies "will always be content to do what lies at hand today." They must not seek to "master and control what things and relations will be in the future."[57]

The justified advance no claim to totality in what they do. On the contrary, they can be extremely skeptical about such claims because their justification does not depend upon success. They are not condemned to success.

Free for Service

Luther speaks as an expositor of Paul when he says that "a man is justified without works — although he does not remain without works when

---

56. WA 15:372,22–373,17; LW 45:331 (translation altered).
57. *Luthers Vorreden zur Bibel,* 81; WADB 10/II:106,9.

he has been justified."[58] "Faith justifies without any works; and yet it does not follow that men are therefore to do no good works, but rather that the genuine works will not be lacking."[59] The law is not abolished; it is fulfilled. All that we do comes from the inner heart. "But such a heart is given only by God's Spirit who fashions a man after the law, so that he acquires a pleasure in the law in his heart, doing nothing henceforth out of fear and compulsion but out of a willing heart."[60]

Luther never tires of emphasizing the freedom and spontaneity of the new obedience, how the regenerate listen and act. At issue here is the faith that works by love.[61] He handles the relationship of faith and love in his *Freedom of a Christian* under the twofold heading that "a Christian is a perfectly free lord of all, subject to none. A Christian is a perfectly dutiful servant of all, subject to all."[62] Christians are not a separate species of human beings, not even of religious human beings, but human as such, liberated humans. In faith they live outside themselves in God, freed from having to find their own identity or achieve self-fulfillment. For this reason they can afford to be the servants not merely of all people but of all things, thus caring for them "as if there were no God."

Throughout his tractate on freedom, Luther is simply expounding the saying of Paul in 1 Corinthians 9:19: "For though I am free with respect to all, I have made myself a slave to all." A more precise translation of the Greek reads: Not *though* I am free, but *because* I am free. Luther also claims that he is expounding the passage in Romans 13:8-10 in which Paul refers to love as the fulfilling of the law. With faith we receive freedom for service in love

> so that we have no law nor owe anyone anything except love [Rom. 13:8]. We are to do good things for our neighbors just as Christ has done for us through his blood. Hence all the laws, works, and commandments that are required of us to serve God do not come from

58. *Luthers Vorreden zur Bibel*, 187; WADB 7:16,17-19; LW 35:374.
59. *Luthers Vorreden zur Bibel*, 188; WADB 7:16,35-38; LW 35:374.
60. *Luthers Vorreden zur Bibel*, 179; WADB 7:4,31-34; LW 35:367.
61. See Gal. 5:6, "the only thing that counts is faith working through love."
62. WA 7:21,1-4; LW 31:344; Cl 2:11,6-9; IL I:239.

God. . . . Yet these laws, works, and commandments that are required of us to serve our neighbors are good and we should do them, such as obeying the government of the secular power, following it and serving it, feeding the hungry, helping the needy.[63]

Fulfilling the law in love does not lead us out of the struggle of justifications but plunges us into its depths.[64] Yet the battle between lord and servant for mutual recognition has been decided in a movement that counteracts the deadly battle of world history. The decision was this: God himself who is free from all, in virtue of his riches, became poor for our sakes in the history of Jesus Christ, so that we through his poverty might become rich. This is how Paul, in 2 Corinthians 8:9, describes the event that we know so well from the hymn to Christ in Philippians 2:6-11, and Luther after him. The turning point in the dispute of "justifications" came with the history of Jesus Christ, which — through and beyond the death of the old Adam — retrieves Christians and sets them aright.

> Righteousnesss, then, is such a faith. It is called "the righteousness of God" because God gives it and counts it as righteousness for the sake of Christ our Mediator, and makes a man to fulfill his obligation to everybody. For through faith a man becomes free from sin and comes to take pleasure in God's commandments, thereby he gives God the honor due him, and pays what he owes him. Likewise he serves his fellow-men willingly, by whatever means he can, and thus pays his debt to everyone.[65]

The faith that works and shows its energy by love does not separate itself from the context of the dispute of "justifications" but moves in a certain way within it. The forensic structure of reality — being as judgment, being in mutual recognition — is not abolished but, as we have described it, fulfilled. In this sense the tradition of Old Testament and Near Eastern

---

63. WA 12:157,6-14; IL V:37. Cf. WA 26:505,11-15; LW 37:365; Cl 3:510,34-38; IL II:257.

64. On this and what follows, see Bayer, "Macht, Recht, Gerechtigkeit," *Kerygma und Dogma* 30 (1984): 200ff. esp. 210f.

65. *Luthers Vorreden zur Bibel,* 183; WADB 7:10,28-33; LW 35:371.

wisdom — the world order as communal faithfulness and justice — is caught up under the concept of love and thus brought to fulfillment. This many-sided and even, in itself, dissonant process of tradition has to be seen in its entire context. Luther does not restrict himself to an insular exposition of Paul. That is a common misunderstanding of his theology and of Article IV of the Augsburg Confession. The fact that the law finds fulfillment in love, and righteousness in mercy, leads into the broadest of social and cosmic relationships.

Chapter Four

Faith Comes by Hearing

Delusion and Word

On what does faith live? What distinguishes Luther's view of faith from human delusion and dreaming, from the opinions of those who "by their own powers create an idea in their heart which says, 'I believe,'"[1] whose belief consists of a decision, a giving or finding of meaning for everything?

What differentiates the delusion of all forms of metaphysics and morality, even religious and ecclesiastical forms, from authentic faith? Luther offers only a single answer. Faith comes by listening to preaching. It derives from the Word of God, the external verbal Word. The passive righteousness of faith takes places only in virtue of the Word *(solo verbo)*. What does this mean? We must also find an answer to the much-debated question whether the promised righteousness is just a "forensic" righteousness, the righteousness of a mere verdict, or whether it is really an "effective" righteousness, one that genuinely changes us and truly makes us new.

When Luther describes faith as a "divine work in us" in which God himself slays the old nature that belongs to the old world, the old Adam,

---

1. Cf. WADB 7:8,30f. and 7:10,1-2; LW 35:370; cf. WA 40/II:326,34-37 and 327,13-16; LW 12:310: "This knowledge of sin, moreover, is not some sort of speculation or an idea which the mind thinks up for itself. It is a true feeling, a true experience, and a very serious struggle of the heart, as [the Psalmist] testifies when he says (v. 3), 'I know (that is, I feel or experience) my transgressions.' This is what the Hebrew really means."

and makes us new creatures, a new creation, he is identifying the decisive aspect of the Word that creates justifying faith. For Luther the customary alternative of "forensic" or "effective" is no alternative at all. The forensic is effective, the effective forensic. That is his answer to the much-debated question. What God says, God does. The reverse is also true. What God does, God says; his doing is not ambiguous. God's work is God's speech. God's speech is no fleeting breath. It is a most effective breath that creates life, that summons into life.[2] It is the "nature" of God to create out of nothing, to be the Creator by the Word alone. This is not a speculative thought, for those who confess the one who creates out of nothing and gives life to the dead are those who have experienced the truth that God justifies the ungodly by his Word,[3] creating a new self for the old Adamic self.

Let us look a little more closely at the context *(Sitz im Leben)* in which the ungodly are pronounced to be righteous and are thereby *made* righteous. This declaration does not come directly from heaven, but through another person — in a very creaturely fashion. Another person, speaking in the name and on the commission of God, speaks this promise to me, but this is in fact the speaking and acting of God himself. This Word is the basis of assurance of faith, of newness of life, of belonging to Christ and his history, which means belonging to the new world of God, to God's kingdom, the kingdom which is not about to come but has already come. For the kingdom is present when the Word that makes everything new is heard and believed, when this passive righteousness of faith is imparted and becomes active in love.

What are our lives directed toward? This is the decisive point. It is decisive in the controversy of Luther's theology with Roman Catholicism and with Pietism about that which has been called — differing from Luther's own theology — the question of relating justification and sanctification. To what do we look? May we and can we look away from ourselves and solely at Christ? Or do we look back at ourselves as made anew,

2. See Ps. 33:6, "By the word of the Lord the heavens were made, and all their host by the breath of his mouth."

3. See Rom. 4:17, "the God . . . who gives life to the dead and calls into existence the things that do not exist," and Rom. 4:5, "But to one who without works trusts him who justifies the ungodly, such faith is reckoned righteousness."

seeking to monitor ourselves in the growth of faith and love, in the new obedience, in the progress we make, even in the sanctification that is said to follow after justification? When we are blessed by God and born anew, do we seek to feel the pulse of our own faith? Doing this is a dangerous displacement that leads us away from the Reformation understanding of faith. The moment we turn aside and look back at ourselves and our own doings instead of at God and God's promise, at that moment we are again left alone with ourselves and with our own judgment about ourselves. We will then be inevitably entangled in ourselves. We will fall back into all the uncertainty of the defiant and despairing heart that looks only to self and not to the promise of God. That is why it is so important to take note of the means or medium by which justifying faith comes.

According to Romans 10:17, faith comes by hearing. It comes by hearing the Word that addresses us. It comes in the promise and pro-nouncement by which Jesus Christ opens up himself and the kingdom of God to me, bringing me, within the Christian community, back home, to paradise, and making me a new person. The Augsburg Confession was adopting the theology of Luther when in Article V it spoke about the ministry of the Word — its "institution" — by which we receive justifying faith: "To obtain such faith God instituted the office of preaching, giving the gospel and the sacraments. Through these, as (i.e.) through means, he gives the Holy Spirit who produces faith, where and when he wills, in those who hear the gospel. It teaches us that we have a gracious God, not through our merit but through Christ's merit, when we so believe."[4] The Confession rejects a direct and immediate — an "enthusiastic" — under-standing of the Holy Spirit. It insists on God's coming by means of and within the external Word *(verbum externum),* the bodily Word.

Article V is the most important article in the Confession. It is the de-cisive factor for the understanding of justification in Article IV and of

---

4. *Die Bekenntnisschriften der evangelisch-lutherischen Kirche,* 11th ed. (Göttingen: Vandenhoeck & Ruprecht, 1992), 58, 1-10 [hereafter cited as BSLK]; *The Book of Concord: The Confession of the Evangelical Lutheran Church,* ed. Robert Kolb and Timothy J. Wengert (Minneapolis: Fortress Press, 2000), 40,1-3 [hereafter cited as BC]; *The Book of Concord: The Confessions of the Evangelical Lutheran Church,* ed. and trans. Theodore G. Tappert (Phila-delphia: Fortress Press, 1959), 31 [hereafter cited as BC-T].

good works and the new obedience in Article VI; it tips the balance. The most fundamental of all institutions is the "institution" of the Word itself. The world itself depends on it, not just the church, and certainly not just the territorial or local church. It is the institution and the event out of which faith comes, which enables us to see the world as creation — what is possible only through judgment. From this institution and event derives faith in him "who gives life to the dead and calls into existence the things that do not exist."[5]

Is the Word to be rated that highly? Should we not inquire into its credibility and authority? Must not a material and tangible history stand behind it? Is it not just a witness to an event, from which it must be differentiated? Do we not have to agree with Goethe's Faust that we should "not value the Word so highly"? Should we not correct the first verse of John's Gospel, as Faust did, and say: "In the beginning was the — deed"?

Deed as Word and Word as Deed

Let us pause here to examine more carefully what it means to speak in such fundamental terms about the "Word," as seen above. What sense does it make to speak of the "Word" as the absolute definition of Being?

When Plato refers to what defines Being, he speaks about the "idea." Aristotle talks of "form." Marx, like Bloch, speaks of "labor" as the "self-generation" that brings humanity to its home. Are not the "idea," the "form," and the world's history of "labor" much more comprehensive terms than the oral "Word"?

In answering this question we can first refer to Max Weber's approach to sociology. The theme of sociology is human acting. Only if it is understandable, however, can it be subjected to academic research. It must have a meaning that the investigator can discover. In other words, we must be able to see actions as acts that speak. We normally distinguish words and acts. But if in a certain situation someone throws a cobblestone at a car, no word is necessary; the action "speaks" for itself. Similarly a

5. See note 3.

non-verbal slap in the face is an act that "speaks." Some acts "speak volumes." There are thus problems in distinguishing the sentiment of the heart, the word of the mouth, and the act of the hand. There is, of course, a recognizable distinction between an evil thought that is perhaps concealed, a spoken word that wounds, or an act of murder. At the same time there is a connection between sentiment, word, and act, between heart, mouth, and hand. This connection can be understood as "word." For this reason we must not make too strict a distinction between symbolic and instrumental power. "Pure" deeds also speak, and "pure" words establish facts.

Many situations make it plain that the word is also deed, for example, a statement made at a trial, something said to someone in despair that drives him to suicide by taking away his zest for life, or that works the opposite and gives him new life. A glance or a shrug of the shoulders can also be an act that destroys or renews life. When communion is disrupted by a quarrel, a single glance or word can bring forgiveness. The glance, as an act, is in this case an effective word, a deed.

When we speak of "word" here we are speaking of communication as such. The saying "God created the world by the Word" means simply that God's will is to have communion with us, and with all creatures. We communicate with one another and with the creatures only because communion, loyalty, and justice have been established, promised, and instituted as the order of the world. The coherence and communication of this world and of our own lives are never, not a single moment, in our own hands; rather, they are granted to us. They are granted by a prior and prevenient Word so that we and all creatures can respond to this Word, and to each other, as "day to day pours forth speech."[6]

This response is also an "effective" word. There is nothing magical about it. It is what we find in all our own life histories. We need not think of negligent parents, but of what takes place every day, even if it is not reported in the newspapers: children are wanted and awaited and recognized for the right to live even before they are born, so that from the very first when they come into the world they will know devotion. After all, babies do not enter

6. Ps. 19:2. Cf. Hos. 2:21f.

46

the world smiling. Rather, days and weeks pass before they can recognizably respond. They do so only because others anticipate their love and devotion by smiling at and talking to them. When children are addressed they learn to reply. They learn to hear and to speak in connection with their discovery of their body's abilities. By "grasping," thinking and doing are formed simultaneously. From the very beginning human speech is permeated by physicality. Gestures and speech are so interwoven that our very faces "speak." Word and body, word and action are so bound up together that they cannot be separated. Our Western philosophical tradition has given the *intellect* prominence among our human faculties. Luther, however, says that "there is no mightier or nobler work of man than *speech*."[7] We are not rational beings first of all; we are primarily speaking beings. Because this is so, we can understand that the deed of God occurs as word and the word as deed.[8] As speaking beings we can understand the references to God's "bodily Word," as in Article V of the Augsburg Confession.

Word and Authority of the Bible

If, like Luther and the Augsburg Confession, we regard the "bodily Word" as central, then we have to investigate our understanding of the authority of the Bible and its relationship to the justifying Word.

Luther reads, hears, and understands the Bible as witness to the living Word and as itself a living Word which addresses us bodily, "externally"[9] — I can hear it, and therefore sing and speak of it. For Luther everything depends upon the Bible; hearing, using, and preaching it as the living voice of the gospel (*viva vox evangelii*). This is for him no mere

---

7. Luther, "Zweite Vorrede auf den Psalter" (1528), in *Luthers Vorreden zur Bibel,* 66; WADB 10/I:100,12-14; LW 35:254.

8. The theology of the Word thus has an anthropological basis, for "it is a special gift of God that he lends us speech, and that is why he had given his external Word to the churches." WATR 4:122,27-30 (No. 4081).

9. Cf. Article 27 of the *Confessio Virtembergica,* which describes holy Scripture as "a true and certain preaching of the Holy Spirit." "Confessio Virtembergica. Das württembergische Bekenntnis von 1551," E. Bizer, ed., *Blätter für württembergische Kirchengeschichte* (Sonderheft) 7 (1952): 178.

matter of thought. It is not a proposition; instead, we have here a "voice that comes to us."[10] Hence he can say that God has not fixed his Word in dead books but in the living voice[11] that we hear in its materiality. This voice is not a passing breath that perhaps is the occasion of an inward recollection of something which has supposedly always been there and which one can therefore recognize.[12] Luther does not see it this way at all.

Since God has given us his Word in a living voice, we can see why Luther, although intensively concerned with the text and every letter of the Bible, rates the oral character of the Word more highly than its written form.[13] The importance of the oral and public character of the Word is finely portrayed in his *Short Instruction About What We Are to Expect in the Gospels.*[14] We read there about Christ, that it is through preaching the gospel that "Christ comes to us, or we are brought to him."[15] Communication takes place. The gospel "signifies nothing else than a sermon or report concerning the grace and mercy of God merited and acquired through the Lord Jesus Christ with his death. Actually, the Gospel is not what one finds in books and what is written in letters of the alphabet; it is rather an oral sermon and a living Word, a voice that resounds throughout the world and is proclaimed publicly, so that one hears it everywhere."[16]

In his 1522 *Preface to the New Testament* Luther speaks of the oral character of the New Testament in an incomparably impressive way.

> For "gospel" [*Euangelion*] is a Greek word and means in Greek a good message, good tidings, good news, a good report, which one sings and tells with gladness. For example, when David overcame the great Goliath, there came among the Jewish people the good report

10. WADB 6:8,18f.; LW 35:359-60.

11. Cf. WA 5:537,10-22.

12. For Augustine the external Word is a sign *(signum)* that simply points us to the matter *(res)*. This "hermeneutics of signification" finds impressive testimony especially in "de magistro" I.2. Translated and edited by J. Burleigh under the title "The Teacher" in *Augustine: Earlier Writings* (Philadelphia: The Westminster Press, 1953), 70f.

13. WA 5:643,25-29. Cf. Bayer, *Promissio* 249f.; WA 10,I/1:625,12–628,8.

14. WA 10,I/1:8,12–18,3; LW 35:117-24.

15. WA 10,I/1:13,22–14,1; LW 35:121.

16. WA 12:259,8-13; cf. 275, 9-12; LW 30:3.

and encouraging news that their terrible enemy had been struck down and that they had been rescued and given joy and peace; and they sang and danced and were glad for it [1 Sam. 18:6].

Thus this gospel of God or New Testament is a good story and report, sounded forth into all the world by the apostles, telling of a true David who strove with sin, death, and the devil, and overcame them, and thereby rescued all those who were captive in sin, afflicted with death, and overpowered by the devil. Without any merit of their own he made them righteous, gave them life, and saved them, so that they were given peace and brought back to God. For this they sing, and thank and praise God and are glad forever, if only they believe firmly and remain steadfast in faith.

This report and encouraging tidings, or evangelical and divine news, is also called a New Testament. For it is a testament when a dying man bequeaths his property, after his death, to his legally defined heirs. And Christ, before his death, commanded and ordained that his gospel be preached in all the world [Luke 24:44-47]. Thereby he gave to all who believe, as their possession, everything that he had. This included: his life, in which he swallowed up death; his righteousness, by which he blotted out sin; and his salvation, with which he overcame everlasting damnation. A poor man, dead in sin and consigned to hell, can hear nothing more comforting than this precious and tender message about Christ; from the bottom of his heart he must laugh and be glad over it, if he believes it true.[17]

In this understanding of the gospel Luther never *formally* answers the question of the authority of the oral, bodily Word in relation to that of the written word of the Bible. Instead, he offers a very *material* answer by pointing out that the preached Word that comes to us by word of mouth is Jesus Christ himself now present with us. The Word is the "voice [that] says, 'Christ is your own with his life, teaching, works, death, resurrection, and all that he is, has, does, and can do.'"[18]

17. Luther, "Vorrede auf das Neue Testament" (1522) in *Luthers Vorreden zur Bibel,* 168f.; WADB 6:2,23-25; 4:1-23; LW 35:357 (n. 1), 358-59.

18. *Luthers Vorreden zur Bibel,* 171; WADB 6:9,18f.; LW 35:361.

Here, then, is the measure, the canon, of what is absolutely true and truly valid as a justifying Word in the dispute of "justifications."[19]

> All the true and proper sacred writings agree on one point. They all preach and promote Christ. The proper touchstone for evaluating the books is whether we find that they truly promote Christ or not, for all scripture bears witness to Christ [Rom. 3:21] and St. Paul wants to know nothing but Christ [1 Cor. 2:2]. That which does not teach Christ is not apostolic even though it is taught by St. Peter or St. Paul. But whatever preaches Christ is apostolic even though it be done by Judas, Hannan, Pilate, and Herod.[20]

Christ as Bodily Word

If the gospel were not Jesus Christ himself, and therewith the undivided presence of the triune God, it could not be described as the might and power of God as Paul calls it when summarizing it in his letter to the Romans in 1:16f.: "For I am not ashamed of the gospel; it is the power of God for salvation to everyone who has faith, to the Jew first and also to the Greek. For in it the righteousness of God is revealed through faith for faith; as it is written, 'The one who is righteous will live by faith.'" As the "power" of God, the Word of the gospel is none other than the "kingdom of God." The gospel *is* the kingdom. It does not simply proclaim it or point to it; it brings and causes all the hearers, including myself, to enter it. As Jesus Christ, as God himself, the gospel, when preached by word of mouth, does more than simply offer us the possibility that I can actualize and make it real by my own decision of faith. The Word itself *is* the power of God, God's kingdom.[21]

---

19. For many years Protestant theology has inappropriately distinguished between its formal principle (the authority of the Bible) and its material principle (the doctrine of justification). August D. C. Twesten introduced this distinction in 1826. See his *Vorlesungen über die Dogmatik der evangelisch-lutherischen Kirche,* 4th ed., vol. 1, compiled by W. M. L. deWette (Hamburg: Perthes, 1838), 258-60.

20. *Luthers Vorreden zur Bibel,* 216f.; WADB 7:384,25-32.

21. Compare Rom. 1:16f. with 1 Cor. 4:20.

If then, the Word is so significant, great importance attaches to its exact form. It has the form of a promise, as in Isaiah 43:1: "Do not fear, for I have redeemed you; I have called you by name, you are mine," or as in Luke 2:10-11, "Do not be afraid . . . to you is born this day . . . a Savior." The whole Bible, Old Testament as well as New, abounds in such promises. Most important for Luther is the presence of Jesus Christ as the justifying Word of God in the promises at penance, baptism, and the Lord's Supper: "I acquit you of all your sins"; "I baptize you in the name of the Father, the Son, and the Holy Spirit." The meaning is this: "You belong to me, you are in my hands," says God, and therefore "Take and eat, this is my body, given for you! Take and drink, this cup is the new testament in my blood that was shed for the forgiveness of your sins!" To put this briefly, the meaning is: "I am for you." By such a promise God discloses himself as the one who is in communion with us.

The term "promise" *(promissio)* is the center of Luther's theology. When he says that God promises, he does not refer to something in the future that we may anticipate. The promise is not only an announcement that will only be fulfilled in the future. It is a valid and powerful promise and pledge that takes immediate and present effect. A good comparison is the text of English banknotes: "I promise to pay the bearer on demand the sum of X amount of pounds. London, for the governor and company of the Bank of England, Chief Cashier." With this understanding of the term "promise" Luther was moving along the lines of medieval German legal thinking that used the word *promissio* to describe the way a ruler bound and committed himself at his enthronement.[22] This was how God also committed himself in the *promissio* pronounced in his name. He was bound by it and will stick to it and keep it. Faith lays hold of God by accepting and counting on the given promise, and therefore it lays hold of the "faithfulness of God, of his truth, his Word,

22. Cf. Percy E. Schramm, *Geschichte des englischen Königtums im Lichte der Krönung,* 1st edition (Köln/Böhlau/Darmstadt: Wissenschaftliche Buchgesellschaft, 1937, 1970), 179ff. ("vom Mandatum regis zur Promissio regis"); K. Sturm, "Die Dialektik der Rechtfertigungslehre," *Neue Stimme. Evangelische Monatsschrift zu Fragen in Kirche, Gesellschaft und Politik* (n.p., 1978): 13-18.

his righteousness."[23] The truth of faith lies in participation in the promise and faithfulness of God that is promised and imparted to it.

> Truth means faithfulness on which we can rely and in whom we can take refuge, and we ourselves will stand by what we say and live up to what is expected. Thus God everywhere in Scripture glorifies himself regarding us in the fact that he is merciful and faithful, always displaying faithfulness and love and offering us to the full both friendship and blessing. We can rely upon it that he will do this, faithfully fulfilling all that we expect. The Hebrew word for faithfulness and truth is *emeth*. From this comes *emuna,* and quoting Habakkuk, St. Paul translates this as faith [Rom. 1:17]: "The just shall live by faith." The Psalms often speak of the "faith" of God. In his "faith" God gives faith to us and we build upon it. In Hebrew the words "truth" and "faith" or "faithfulness" mean much the same and can be used interchangeably. In our language we say that those who keep the faith are true and trustworthy. Those whom we mistrust we regard as false and untrustworthy.[24]

God keeps his promises. God pledges himself to us. In giving us faith God shows faith in us.[25] The concepts of faith and faithfulness are both present. God pledges himself to us and gives faith to us. Hence we too can have faith in God and rely upon him.

The Triune God

The entire Godhead — Father, Son, and Holy Spirit — communicates and imparts itself to that faith in the promise of God.

23. *Luthers Vorreden zur Bibel,* 70; WADB 10/I:588,19f., particularly on grace and truth (חסד ואמח); cf. *Luthers Vorreden zur Bibel,* 62; cf. Gen. 24:49; 47:29; Exod. 34:6; Josh. 2:14; 2 Sam. 2:6, 15:20; Ps. 25:10, 61:8, 85:11, 86:15; Prov. 3:3, 14:22, 16:6, 20:28.

24. Luther, "Erste Vorrede auf den Psalter" (1524) in *Luthers Vorreden zur Bibel,* 62f.; WADB 10/I:94,22-26; 96,1-9.

25. The German terms for "pledge" [*geloben*] and "have faith" [*glauben*] are etymologically related, sharing the same word root, *gelouben.*

These are the three persons and one God, who has given himself to us all wholly and completely, with all that he is and has. The Father gives himself to us, with heaven and earth and all the creatures, in order that they may serve us and benefit us. But this gift has become obscured and useless through Adam's fall. Therefore the Son subsequently gave himself and bestowed all his works, sufferings, wisdom, and righteousness, and reconciled us to the Father, in order that we, restored to life and righteousness, might also know and have the Father and his gifts.

But because this grace would benefit no one if it remained so profoundly hidden and could not come to us, the Holy Spirit comes and gives himself to us also, wholly and completely. He teaches us to understand this deed of Christ which has been manifested to us, helps us receive and preserve it, use it to our advantage and impart it to others, increase and extend it.[26]

In a dramatic hymn Luther sang of the fact that God's being is gift and promise. This hymn, "Dear Christians, One and All," is the most telling and appropriate confession of the triune God that I know. Other attempts to speak of the triune God switch between the definition of the timeless relationships of Father, Son, and Spirit and the thought that there are successive temporal epochs of their action as Father, as Son, and as Spirit. A third option is to eliminate these extremes by merging speculation and actual history. What does not come to light in these efforts is the fact that God's being is gift and promise as he gives himself wholly and utterly to us.

With this hymn as drama, Luther has God speak to himself and thus also speak for us and to us. What takes place in this drama is our justification. "And you are blest forever" is the conclusion of the eighth verse. Justification comes when God himself enters the deadly dispute of "justifications," suffers from it, carries it out in himself. He does this through the death of his Son, which is also God's own death. In this way God takes the dispute into himself and overcomes it on our behalf.

26. WA 26:505,38–506,7; LW 37:366; Cl 3:511,21-33; IL II:258f.; cf. the summary in the Large Catechism, WA 30/1:192,17-29; WA 4:32-61,6.

1. Dear Christians, one and all, rejoice,
   With exultation springing,
   And, with united heart and voice
   And holy rapture singing,
   Proclaim the wonder God has done,
   How his right arm the vict'ry won,
   What price our ransom cost him!

2. Fast bound in Satan's chains I lay,
   Death brooded darkly o'er me.
   Sin was my torment night and day;
   In sin my mother bore me.
   But daily deeper still I fell;
   My life became a living hell,
   So firmly sin possessed me.

3. My own good works all came to naught,
   No grace or merit gaining;
   Free will against God's judgment fought,
   Dead to all good remaining.
   My fears increased till sheer despair
   Left only death to be my share;
   The pangs of hell I suffered.

4. But God has seen my wretched state
   Before the world's foundation,
   And, mindful of his mercies great,
   He planned for my salvation.
   He turned to me a father's heart;
   He did not choose the easy part,
   But gave his dearest treasure.

5. God said to his beloved Son:
   "'Tis time to have compassion.
   Then go, bright jewel of my crown,
   And bring to all salvation;
   From sin and sorrow set them free;

Slay bitter death for them that they
May live with you forever."

6. The Son obeyed his Father's will,
   Was born of a virgin mother;
   And, God's good pleasure to fulfill,
   He came to be my brother.
   His royal pow'r disguised he bore,
   A servant's form, like mine, he wore,
   To lead the devil captive.

7. To me he said: "Stay close to me,
   I am your rock and castle.
   Your ransom I myself will be;
   For you I strive and wrestle;
   For I am yours and you are mine,
   And where I am you may remain;
   The foe shall not divide us.

8. "Though he will shed my precious blood,
   Of life me thus bereaving,
   All this I suffer for your good;
   Be steadfast and believing.
   Life will from death the vict'ry win;
   My innocence shall bear your sin;
   And you are blest forever.

9. "Now to my Father I depart,
   From earth to heav'n ascending,
   And heav'nly wisdom to impart,
   The Holy Spirit sending;
   In trouble he will comfort you
   And teach you always to be true
   And into truth shall guide you.

10. "What I on earth have done and taught
    Guide all your life and teaching;

So shall the Kingdom's work be wrought
And honored in your preaching.
But watch lest foes with base alloy
The heav'nly treasure should destroy;
This final word I leave you."[27]

The praise of the congregation in verse 1 is an answer given to the laments of our old and lost nature in verses 2-3.[28] It is the self-giving and self-committing of the triune God. It is stated in such a way that those who cry from the depths of hell are heard, and hearing they are received from the outset into the inner divine discourse. The dialogue between the Father and the Son, the Son and the Father is no speculative construct in trinitarian theology but an event that applies to sinners from the very first, recounted as "mercies great." The whole being of God is understood as a self-giving promise that is made to us by the Son in our lost estate when we were given over to death: "Stay close to me. . . . Your ransom I myself will be" (verses 7-10).

What a promise is this! It must surely cause us to sing. As Luther says, "God has cheered our hearts and minds through his dear Son, whom he gave for us to redeem us from sin, death, and the devil. He who believes this earnestly cannot be quiet about it. But he must gladly and willingly sing and speak about it so that others also may come and hear it."[29]

The story and promise described in the hymn that tell us to "stay close" to God do not belong to Martin Luther alone. Many thousands joined his song and found in the turning point of Luther's life the watershed of their own lives. Albrecht Dürer, for one, bears witness that Luther with his reformation words "helped me out of great distress."[30]

Luther's anxieties were those of a whole epoch. It is thus understandable that this liberation had an epochal effect. What one person,

27. Luther, "Nun freut euch, lieben Christen g'mein," EG #341. Translated by Richard Massie under the title "Dear Christians, One and All," LBW, #299.

28. Cf. Rom. 7:24.

29. WA 35:477,6-9; LW 53:333; IL V:285.

30. Albrecht Dürer in a letter to Spalatin early in 1520. Albrecht Dürer, 32nd Letter, in *Autobiographische Schriften; Briefwechsel; Dichtungen,* vol. 1 of *Schriftlicher Nachlass,* ed. H. Rupprich (Berlin: Deutscher Verlag für Kunstwissenschaft, 1956), 66f.

deeply troubled by the judgment of God, found as the answer to the question of grace, became for many others the basis and confession of their own faith. The answer was, of course, also misunderstood and misused. Luther had hardly begun to proclaim the freedom of a Christian before he had to fight against abuse of the term. He did not do this in such a way as to speak about the good works that must be added to faith. Instead, he did so by calling people back to that faith that occurs "where the Holy Spirit gives people faith in Christ and thus sanctifies them."[31]

31. WA 50:626,20f.; LW 41:145.

Chapter Five

Faith and Sanctification

In our modern age, influenced by Pietism and the Enlightenment, our thinking is shaped by what is subjective, by the life of faith, by our inner disposition and motivation, by our inward impulses and the way they are shaped. When we think and live along these lines, sanctification is a matter of personal and individual development and orientation. It is true that we also find this approach in Luther. No one emphasized more sharply than he did our personal responsibility and irreplaceability. But this approach is secondary. "The Word of God always comes first. After it follows faith; after faith, love; then love does every good work, for . . . it is the fulfilling of the law."[1]

Luther understands sanctification as the work of God the Holy Spirit. He speaks of it in what we would call an objective fashion. This is the special focus in the explanation of the third article of the Creed in the Large Catechism and also in the 1539 work, *On the Councils and the Church.* Especially in reference to this work, we face the question of the relation between justification and sanctification in both the ongoing debate between Protestantism and Roman Catholicism and also in the ongoing debate within Protestantism itself, namely Pietism, Methodism, and the Holiness Movement. Luther himself did not raise this question, since for him justification by faith alone meant that everything was said and done; living by faith is already the new life. When, nevertheless, Lu-

1. WA 6:514,19f.; LW 36:39; Cl 1:445,30-32.

ther speaks about "sanctification" he simply talks about justification. Justification and sanctification are not for him two separate acts that we can distinguish, as though sanctification follows after justification, and has to do so. In talking about sanctification Luther stresses the institutional side of the event of justification. In keeping with the first and second tables of the decalogue he differentiates the spiritual and the secular "regime and government" of God,[2] the church belonging both to the spiritual realm and to the secular just as well.

Communion of Saints

The starting point for Luther is the New Testament description of Christians as saints, as those who are "called" by God the Holy Spirit.[3] In the work, *On the Councils and the Church,* in which the theme of sanctification is stressed, there is an express discussion of the question of the nature of the Church in terms of the work of the Spirit on human hearts, souls, bodies, works, and our human nature. In both tables of the law the Holy Spirit is at work, giving vitality and holiness to our whole being. The marks of the Church are the means of sanctification, through which the Holy Spirit sanctifies his people according to the first table. Clearly those who are sanctified by the work of Christ, the forgiveness of sins, are now placed in his discipleship. Nevertheless, the focus is not upon the saints but upon sanctification, upon the Word of God in all its sacramental forms, and also upon secular institutions that correspond to the second table of the law. When we are sanctified, the meaning is that God himself sanctifies us by imparting himself to us as the Holy One, who alone is holy. Only God is holy, and what he says and speaks and does is holy. This is how God's holiness works, which he does not keep to himself, but communicates by sharing it.

The decisive thing that in all respects defines holiness and sanctification is the sacred Word of God. "This," says Luther, "is the principal

2. WA 50:652,29; LW 41:177; IL V:220.
3. Cf., e.g., 1 Cor. 1:2.

59

item, and the holiest sanctuary, by reason of which the Christian people are called holy; for God's Word is holy and sanctifies everything it touches."[4] This holy and sanctifying Word of God is first of all the oral Word. According to Luther "we also speak of this oral and external Word as it is sincerely believed and openly professed before the world."[5]

Sanctified by the Divine Word of Institution

In a way that seems strange to us, Luther talks of sanctification not merely *in* institutions but also *through* institutions. Along these lines he speaks of the three "estates," the three basic forms of life into which God's promise has disposed us, the Church, the economy, and the political sphere. Everything natural and everything cultural, the whole world in all the width and depth of its inner and outer nature, all social relationships and our relationship to self, stand under the Word of God that "sanctifies" these relationships, or "institutions."

Luther's doctrine of the three estates is not very well known. Yet he regards it as so highly significant that he can find in it the first rule of biblical exposition. In his *Table Talk* from the winter of 1542/43 he says that there are three rules for translating the Bible. The first is that "the Bible speaks and teaches about the works of God. About this there can be no doubt. These works are divided in the three estates: the household, the government, the church."[6] These three estates are for Luther the only means by which God sanctifies us in our everyday world. Luther says this with the utmost seriousness in the presence of God and humans in his confession of 1528, which until his dying day remained his irrevocable will and testament, his summarized legacy. According to this statement the three estates are constituted by God's Word and command. "And whatever is constituted by God's Word must be holy, for

4. WA 50:629,2f.; LW 41:149; IL V:189; cf. the 1528 *Confession Concerning Christ's Supper* (see note 7).
5. WA 50:629,20f.; LW 41:149-50; IL V:189.
6. WATR 5:5533; LW 54:446.

God's Word is holy and sanctifies everything connected with it and involved in it."[7]

The "Three Estates" as Basic Forms of Life

The doctrine of the three estates is the way in which Luther expounds for his own day the Bible's primordial narrative from the standpoint of a theology of creation, of sin, and also of social ethics. The most pregnant summary of his mature understanding may be found in his 1535 exposition of Genesis 2:16-17. He speaks here of three basic forms of life that are God's disposition for humanity. Following tradition, he uses the word "estates" for these forms, a usage which is no longer familiar to us.

The basic estate is that of those whom God addresses and destines for free and thankful response. Our humanity consists of the fact that we are addressed and therefore can hear and can ourselves answer, being responsible for doing so. In the divine address, and the expectation of a human response, there lies the basic process of the cultus, of the worship of God, of the Church, and of religion, all understood as an ordinance of creation. All people and all religions, even atheists, belong to the Church as an ordinance of creation. Every human person belongs as a person to the Church — this defines one's humanity — as an ordinance of creation, a Church, to be sure, which is corrupted by human ingratitude and sin, is perverted and ruined.[8]

Embedded within the basic estate of the Church, of the Word and belief or (in its corrupted form) unbelief — penetrated and embraced by it — is the creation ordinance of the household estate, the economy. Luther discusses here the relation between parents and children, between husbands and wives, but also between humans and agriculture, namely work: our dealings with nature, the procuring of daily bread and means of

7. WA 26:505,8-10; LW 37:365; Cl 3:510,30f.; IL II:257f. Cf. Bayer, "Natur und Institution. Luthers Dreiständelehre, Freiheit als Antwort" (Tübingen: Mohr Siebeck, 1995), 116-46; translated by Luis Dreher as "Nature and Institution: Luther's Doctrine of the Three Orders," *Lutheran Quarterly* 12 (1998): 125-59.
8. Cf. Rom. 1:18-3:20; 1 Cor. 1:18-2:16; John 1:1-18.

life — all this within the compass of his exposition of the petition for daily bread in the Small Catechism.

The third estate, that of politics, was not fully acknowledged by Luther as an ordinance of creation but was rather an emergency ordinance made necessary by the fall. Yet Luther knew, of course, that politics is rooted in economics and should be considered as an implication of the household. In that sense it belongs to the creation ordinance of the household and its regimen.

The fall produced not only the state that upholds the law by methods of compulsion. Even the two unambiguous creation ordinances, the Church and the household or economy, were both radically corrupted by sin. But although thus perverted, they were not destroyed. The promise of God embraces them even in their corruption, and therefore sanctifies them. It is still true, notwithstanding their corruption, that the power of God's creative and pardoning Word may be seen and believed in them. The work of Jesus Christ is to restore creation, to validate again its original purpose, the will of God in creation, as in the relationship of husband and wife. In this, Jesus Christ is the "mediator of creation," through whom all that now is was made.[9] Since sin radically corrupted everything, the deliverance accomplished by Jesus Christ is the only way to salvation. Even the institutions sanctified by God can therefore never be the path to salvation, and even though they are and remain holy, in them we may either be lost or we may find deliverance — by faith alone.[10]

"Hope for Better Times"

It is important that we pay attention to the three estates as the place of sanctification and the sphere of responsibility so that Luther's understanding is not concealed and distorted by too great a concern for the individual and too narrow a view of justification and sanctification. Ac-

9. See John 1:3, "All things came into being through him, and without him not one thing came into being."
10. WA 26:505,11-21; LW 37:365; Cl 3:510,34–511,4; IL II:257f.

cording to Luther we cannot deal with the themes of justification and sanctification without raising and answering the question of the sanctity of institutions and the manner in which they are sanctified by the Word of God. Precisely in terms of the doctrine of the three estates as the place and sphere of sanctification, which is identical with justification, can we understand Luther's concept of growth, of progress in sanctification, and his understanding of history — in which a broad sense of responsibility for the world is needed.

The sanctification of the world was also an important concern for Pietism. Already for Philipp Jakob Spener,[11] the regeneration and renewal of individuals, of Christians, was set within the context of an expected renewal of the whole Church. Since the 1675 *Pia desideria, The Heartfelt Desire for a God-pleasing Reform of the True Evangelical Church,* Spener speaks about the "hope for better times."[12] Primarily he has in view better times for the Church: the forward movement and history of the Church, especially in its relation to the Jews, its missionary task, and its diaconate.[13] In this connection there is also a chiliastic or millennialistic hope, the expectation of a thousand-year kingdom, as in Revelation 20. Spener differed at this point from what Article XVII of the Augsburg Confession says about the return of Christ to judgment. Efforts were made to bridge over the difference by distinguishing between a "crass" and a "subtle" chiliasm. Whether and how this hope of the Pietists was the cause or presupposition of the secular philosophical and political

---

11. Philipp Jakob Spener is "the theologian in whom the Old Protestantism turned to the New Protestantism. Between the Reformation and the nineteenth century there was no other German theologian who equaled him in influence." Johannes Wallmann, "Überlegungen und Vorschläge zu einer Edition des Spenerschen Briefwechsels," *Hoffnung der Kirche und Erneuerung der Welt. Festschrift für Andreas Lindt,* ed. Alfred Schindler (Göttingen: Vandenhoeck & Ruprecht, 1985), 345.

12. This phrase, which is commonly used to interpret the middle section of the *Pia desideria,* was introduced by Spener himself only in the *Behauptung der Hoffnung Künfftiger Besserer Zeiten* (1693), as Johannes Wallmann pointed out to me.

13. Philipp Jakob Spener, *Pia desideria oder herzliches Verlangen nach gottfälliger Besserung der wahren evangelischen Kirche,* 3rd ed., edited by Kurt Aland (Berlin: de Gruyter, 1964), 13ff. Translated by Theodore G. Tappert under the title *Pia desideria* (Philadelphia: Fortress, 1964), 76ff. The phrase in the English is "possibility of better conditions."

hopes, such as we find in Marxism, is a highly interesting and stimulating question that calls for separate treatment.

Luther's view of time, however, stands opposed to such a concept of linear development. Instead, the pivotal point is the distinctive combination and interweaving in which Luther perceives simultaneously the last judgment, the consummation of the world, and creation. He perceives the world and himself with a peculiar overlapping and intertwining of the times such as we find in Romans 8:19-23. The future of the world emerges from God's presence. God's new creation makes the existing world old and restores the original world. The salvation that God imparts today guarantees the approaching consummation of the world and enables us to experience with sorrow the contradiction between the suffering and sighing creatures of the old world and the creation that is promised, the original world.[14]

Metaphysical Progress?

It is difficult for us — influenced as we are by the legacy of Pietism — to think of the world and its history in this way. According to our obstinate misunderstanding, based upon our modern presuppositions, any talk about God's preservation of creation is hard to relate to talk about the future that we can expect from God, if not totally in contradiction to it. And yet this misunderstanding can be resolved. It results from the way that the term "creation" tends to focus one's view back to an absolute beginning, which is then opposed to the orientation toward an absolute goal of a pure future, to promote progressive tendencies that are contrary to restorative ones. This latter orientation has been normative since the French Revolution, and is directly opposed by the understanding of creation that Luther learned from the Bible. Our modern understanding and theology of time fails to see the distinctive intertwining of the times that characterizes the theology of both Paul and Luther. The future of

14. Cf. Oswald Bayer, *Schöpfung als Anrede,* "Zugesagte Welt in der Verschränkung der Zeiten. Luthers Verständnis der Schöpfung," 46-61, and "Tempus creatura verbi," 128-29.

the world derives from the present-day newness of the presence of God; the new creation now disclosed in Baptism and the Lord's Supper turns the old, perverted world into the past and restores the original world as creation.

This intertwining of non-simultaneous times is hard to conceive of, and also more especially, to live in. A linear concept of time is understandably more congenial to us — a universal chronology, a construction of history such as we find in J. A. Bengel,[15] or alternatively an isolation of the "now," of the "moment," of the leap of "decision," as in Søren Kierkegaard or Rudolf Bultmann. But Luther does not opt for this non-expandable moment. Nor does his own chronological ordering of time make history transparent for him. The key to the world does not lie in the number, as in Bengel, but in the promise of God. For this reason Luther's theology is unyielding towards speculations of unity from the standpoint of a theology or philosophy of history. The gap between Luther on the one side and Bengel and Hegel and their theological successors on the other can never be bridged.

Ethical Progress

Luther's understanding of creation and history is opposed to any philosophy of history, and especially to the modern concept of progress. This does not mean, however, that justification places us in a circle in which we can take no firm steps in a specific direction. The exact opposite is the case. In the relation of our new nature to the old we do make progress. In his *Freedom of the Christian* Luther says that we begin and "make some progress in that which shall be perfected in the future life."[16]

Progress is, to be sure, made in the ethical sphere, in the area of works, in our actions, in our political involvement. But it is not absolute

15. Johann Albrecht Bengel, *Ordo temporum* (Stutgardiae: Christoph Erhard, 1741). See also Gerhard Sauter, "Die Zahl als Schlüssel zur Welt. J. A. Bengels 'prophetische Zeitrechnung' im Zusammenhang seiner Theologie," *Evangelische Theologie* 26 (1966): 1-36.

16. WA 7:59,31; LW 31:358. Cf. WA 7:30,5f; Cl 2:36f.; IL I.251f. Cf. "De homine" (1536) and "Disputatio on Romans 3:28" (1537) Theses 17ff., WA 39/I:203.

progress. It is ethical progress without metaphysical pressure. We do not merit the kingdom of God by working for it. It has long since been prepared.[17] The concept of progress is no longer a salvation concept. It loses the religious fascination that it has as a perverted salvation concept. It also loses its fanaticism in the area of politics. As ethical progress, progress divorced from the question of salvation is really secular progress. It is never absolute and total. Instead, it takes place in small but definite steps.

A truly secular progress is "satisfied in doing what lies at hand." It never tries to "master and control the future" of things and relationships in a final way.[18]

Our modern age has forgotten the distinction between ethical and metaphysical progress. We need to ask whether and how far Pietism and Revivalism have contributed to that as well. If the distinction between ethical and metaphysical progress is forgotten, then the significance of Baptism is forgotten as well.

Baptism marks the intersection of the old world and the new. Ethical progress is only possible by returning to Baptism.[19] That progress which will promise us good things, and not just good things but the very best, is a converting and returning to Baptism, and therefore to a new perception of the world in which we no longer have to choose between optimism and pessimism, between shrill anxiety about the future and euphoric hope regarding the further evolution of the cosmos and the enhancement of its possibilities; all the same it remains true that God the Creator unceasingly does new things. Luther's distinctive courage, which goes beyond optimism and pessimism, is grounded in Baptism. It may be seen in a saying that was not his own, although it fits his understanding very well: "Even though the world perish tomorrow, today I will still plant a little apple tree."[20]

In this saying, faith in God the Creator and hope that this world will

---

17. See Matt. 25:34, "inherit the kingdom prepared for you from the foundation of the world."

18. Cf. *Luthers Vorreden zur Bibel,* 80f.; WADB 10/II:106,6-15. See p. 36 above.

19. Cf. WA 6:572,16f. and 528,8-19; LW 36:124 and 59-60; Cl 1:510,38 and 461,20-34.

20. Martin Schloemann, *Luthers Apfelbäumchen? Ein Kapitel deutscher Mentalitätsgeschichte seit dem zweiten Weltkrieg* (Göttingen: Vandenhoeck & Ruprecht, 1994).

perish in its perversion and that grace will finally triumph are all combined. With this faith and hope we need not flee from the present-day twilight between creation and consummation into the supposed clarity of a "hope for better times" in this world's history. Much in the same spirit as Martin Luther, Johann Georg Hamann tells us that the future of the Lord "will come as a thief in the night and therefore there is no time for either political arithmetic or prophetic chronology to bring light."[21]

Law and Gospel

In that skepticism regarding both the Enlightenment's thoughts of progress and the many forms in which Pietism strove after holiness in working for the kingdom, we are to live our lives in history in such a way that we have a distinct knowledge of the difference between law and gospel. In dealing with the relation of justification and sanctification and asking about the validity of the law for the regenerate, the *Formula of Concord,* the Lutheran Confession of 1577, states that "from the beginning of the world these two proclamations have been set forth alongside each other in the church of God with the proper distinction between them. . . . Until the end of the world they must continually be taught in the church of God."[22]

Luther himself continually stressed the fact that the law should not be preached to Christians insofar as they are justified by the gospel. But it should be preached to them insofar as they are sinners and still belong to the old world. This truth finds the same emphasis in Article VI of the *Formula of Concord,* which emphatically seeks to clarify "what the gospel does, effects, and creates for the new obedience of the believers and what the law does in relationship to the good works of believers." This Lutheran confession constantly comes back to our old nature when stressing the validity of the law. For "the old Adam . . . still clings to" the Christian.

21. Johann G. Hamann, *Briefwechsel,* ed. W. Ziesemer and A. Henkel, vol. 4 (Wiesbaden: Insel-Verlag, 1959), 315, 3-5 [text altered].

22. *Formula of Concord,* Article V, BSLK, 959,33–960,1 and 960,23-26. The quotations that follow are taken from 965,30-34; 964,39-42; 969,15f., 44f.; 967,25; 968,1; BC, 585,23 and 586,24; BC-T, 562.

This old Adam is a simple, quarrelsome, "stubborn, recalcitrant donkey" that always wages war against our new nature. There is no real difference between a justified Christian insofar as he still is the old human and an unbelieving and unrepentant non-Christian! The one law is for believers no less than unbelievers.[23]

A particularly important question in our modern nexus of problems, and one that figures today in our peace discussions, is how sanctification, in the spontaneity of new obedience, can be protected from becoming enthusiastic and fanatic. To resolve this question, it is not sufficient to refer only to the ongoing significance of the law for our old nature. We must, with the same seriousness, point to the gospel, give it the priority. If our new nature is to be related to the old, it must in the first place, of course, continue to live. This means, however, that we are continually referred to the pronouncement of the gospel and therefore to the "alien" righteousness that is given to us in Christ. This righteousness is appropriated and imparted. But it is never our own. We could never think of it or recollect it of ourselves. This kind of self-reference, even on the part of those who are devout and want to observe their growth in faith and love, is in constant contradiction of the communion that the gospel grants to us.

In order that those who are renewed and regenerated do not in arrogant or despairing introspection refer again to themselves, we need not only the law that punishes and slays this kind of self-will, but especially also the gospel that prevents this from happening. The spontaneity of the new obedience is protected against enthusiasm by not claiming individualistically and egotistically in blinded self-conceit that it is our own possession, but by taking this spontaneity as the gift of another, by whose power we are enabled to live by faith.

23. BSLK, 965,11f.; 967,18f.; 969,24f.; BC, 589,10; 590,19; 591,24; BC-T, 566, 567, 568.

Chapter Six

Faith within the Lawsuit
about God — Before God

Testing and Lament

In their journey through the world — as pilgrims on the way — believers live under constant test, temptation, challenge, and attack [*Anfechtung*]. The stronger the promise and expectation, the deeper and more passionate the lament, the question of Psalm 22:1, "Why?" Faced with what daily contradicts God's promise of life that is valid for all creatures, the pressing question arises: Is God keeping his promises?[1] God has promised to hear us, but in confronting this promise, the distress is particularly painful — the distress of injustice, of innocent suffering, of hunger, murder, and death.

Lament is only possible because of the promise that it will be heard. Without promise there is no cause for lamentation. Job can only address and challenge the One who in incomprehensible darkness is opposite him, can only bring to this One his lament, protest, and lawsuit, because this One had once made himself audible and listens now in hiddenness. When Eastern European Jews in their worship issue a loud cry to God to respond to his hurting creation and to justify himself, they presuppose that God is listening. This presupposition still lies behind the moral indignation for which the biblical question "why must the righteous suffer?" became the "rock of atheism." This is how Georg Büchner describes

---

1. Cf. WATR 1:69,26–70,9 (no. 148); LW 54:21 (see ch. 1, note 10).

it in Act III of *Dantons Tod:* "Why do I suffer? This is the rock of atheism. The slightest spasm of pain, just one atom, causes a rent in creation that runs from top to bottom."[2]

Those who believe in God's promise and live in the institutions that God's Word has sanctified do not deny that there is a "rent" in God's creation "that runs from top to bottom." They experience it as a contradiction of the world that was promised, of the creation that is "very good."[3] They do not ignore it. The pain that they feel, however, does not make them ungodly and unfeeling people who no longer cry to God. Instead, they dispute with God as Job did, who no longer thought "of God as God but saw only a judge and angry tyrant who acted with violence and never considered the good we did. The only ones who can understand this are those who experience and feel what it means to suffer the wrath and judgment of God and the fact that his grace is hidden."[4]

God's Hiddenness

Luther never downplays or treats as harmless the situation of temptation and testing when God withdraws and conceals himself. He confronts it in all its depth and sharpness. He does not ignore experiences of suffering. Yet he still refuses to accept their finality. He flees from the hidden God to the revealed and incarnate God. He presses on "towards God and even against him calls upon him."[5]

The hidden God is both inaccessibly distant and obtrusively close at the same time. "He has never defined himself by his word." Rather, "God hidden in his majesty neither deplores nor takes away death, but works

2. Georg Büchner, *Dantons Tod,* in *Dantons Tod oder Die Trauerarbeit im Schönen: ein Theater Lesebuch,* ed. Peter von Becker (Frankfurt am Main: Syndikat, 1980), 51. Translated by Hedwig Rappolt under the title *Danton's Death* (New York: TSL, 1980), 167.

3. See Gen. 1:31, "God saw everything that he had made, and indeed, it was very good."

4. Luther, "Vorrede über das Buch Hiob" (1524) in *Luthers Vorreden zur Bibel,* 60; WADB 10/I:4,24-28.

5. WA 19:223,15f. (on Jonah 2:2, 1526); cf. WA 5:204,26f. *(ad deum contra deum confugere).*

life, death, and all in all."[6] In God's overwhelmingly inconceivable hiddenness, God can only be lamented. Lament is an eminent way of perceiving and experiencing the world. For it never surrenders the faith that the creation is "very good," nor does it make evil and suffering harmless, regarding them as nothing. In lament pain is felt in all its profundity. Our most profound testing is that God, who has promised us life and eternal communion, who has guaranteed them, is still the God who does not lament death or destroy it, but who is at work in life and death and all things.

When Luther distinguishes the "hidden" God and the "revealed" God, his approach is in no way speculative, nor is it a means to make the intolerable tolerable, to show that suffering has meaning. The direct setting *(Sitz im Leben)* for talk about the hidden God is lament. Testing and temptation force us to cry to the hidden God in the form of lamentation.

The Promised Answer

The cry of such lament is not a primal human phenomenon like the inarticulate shriek of pain that we share with other creatures. Our scream of indignation and accusation presupposes a disappointed expectation. To suffer injustice, one must know what justice is. The right to life — when withdrawn or attacked — cries out, because the One who gave it hears us. The Judge is the Creator. As Genesis 4:10 states, "Listen; your brother's blood is crying out to me from the ground!" The author of Psalm 9:12 says, "For he who avenges blood is mindful of them; he does not forget the cry of the afflicted."

Distress does not always teach us to pray. It can push us into unlamenting resignation, or despair, or autonomous attempts to overcome it. It does not necessarily lead to lament in the presence of God. The

---

6. WA 18:685,22f.; LW 33:140; Cl 3:177,35-39. The LW translates the WA Latin, "Neque enim tum verbo suo definivit sese" as "he has not bound himself by his word." Cf. Ps. 13 and Jonah 2:3-10, Lam. 3:37f.; Amos 3:6; Isa. 45:7; see also Isa. 45:15 in contrast to 45:19.

Word must come first, to empower us. "To you, O my heart, he has said, 'seek my face!'"[7] Lament and petitionary prayer are possible only on the basis of the promise. "Call on me in the day of trouble; I will deliver you."[8] God is he who addresses and hears us, and he has answered even before we call upon him. "Before they call I will answer."[9]

Only in virtue of the preceding Word and the preceding answer does temptation teach us to pay attention to the Word. Because of the preceding answer, lament under assault drives us to grasp the hidden God at the point where God lets himself be grasped, namely, in the Word of his promise. We can hear and taste the promise in a very condensed form in the Lord's Supper.[10] The Lord of the feast is the crucified One. He tasted death,[11] and recounts it, and as the Living One has the final Word by virtue of his death. Thus, in the midst of life, as the communion feast perceives it, suffering and death are not excluded. Our daily bread includes them. The gift-word of the Lord's Supper, in which God offers himself completely as God does in all other preaching too, evokes "eucharist," thanksgiving and joy. Out of it comes a new turning to our fellow creatures with a distinctive courage. The faith which is "daring confidence in the grace of God makes us merry and bold and happy with all creatures."[12] The courage is that of expectation of the redemption of all things through judgment and death. In the promise of this courage, God reveals himself as the inconceivable Liberator.

To us as pilgrims on the way, the hiddenness and overwhelmingly

---

7. Ps. 27:8. The NRSV reads, "'Come,' my heart says, 'seek his face!' Your face, Lord, do I seek." The German translation of the Hebrew by Luther reads as follows: "Mein Herz hält dir vor dein Wort: 'Ihr sollt mein Antlitz suchen.' Darum suche ich auch, Herr, dein Antlitz."

8. Ps. 50:15.

9. Isa. 65:24.

10. In the catechism of Johannes Brenz the Lord's Supper is introduced with the following question: "How is our faith strengthened in adversity and comforted in temptation? Answer: By the supper of our Lord Jesus Christ." Cf. Christoph Weismann, *Eine kleine Biblia. Die Katechismen von Luther und Brenz. Einführung und Texte* (Stuttgart: Calwer Verlag, 1985), 114.

11. See Heb. 2:9, "that he might taste death for everyone."

12. *Luthers Vorreden zur Bibel,* 183; WADB 7:10,17-19.

inconceivable concealment of God is still a matter of lament. We cannot justify this concealment. It can be set aside neither in existence nor thought, not even by such seductive efforts as that of the later philosophy of Friedrich W. J. Schelling, who did try to take with philosophical seriousness the power of evil. In his attempt to justify evil as a necessary element in God's self-development, evil became a principle. What Luther says about the hidden God is completely opposed to that.

The decisive question here is whether justifying faith and the hope it includes ultimately set out from our human entanglement and entrapment, that is, whether they emerge out of negativity and evil, or whether, out of God's promised goodness, evil is suffered and battled, and despair is endured with hope.

"Negative Dialectic"

Christian theology is self-destructive if it does not speak first and last about the good, if it rather attempts to start with the experiences of what is negative and cherishes Adorno's despairing hope, namely, that "when we take a full look at completed negativity it might come together into the mirror image of its opposite." Adorno concludes his *Reflections from a Damaged Life* with this despairing hope that evil will turn into good.[13]

If there is here no positive encounter with the goodness of God, if no place is found for it in worldly experience, if it is encountered only in the negative that cries out for it, then it is only present as a goodness that is both denied and demanded. The goodness and righteousness of God amount then to nothing more than a pure postulate of practical reason. They are then a demand, in the face of which, as Adorno says, "the question of the reality or unreality of redemption is almost an indifferent one." It then becomes clear what is meant by the subjective mode which Adorno uses: "Philosophy, as it can only be advocated when facing de-

13. Theodor W. Adorno, *Minima Moralia: Reflexionen aus dem beschädigten Leben* (Frankfurt: Suhrkamp Verlag, 1973), 334. Translated by E. F. N. Jephcott under the title *Minima Moralia: Reflections from a Damaged Life* (London: New Left Books, 1974). The quotations in the following paragraph come from the final aphorism, "Zum Ende," 333f.

spair, would be the attempt to look at things as they might be seen from the standpoint of redemption. There is no light in knowledge except for that which shines upon the world from redemption."

The "negative dialectic" of Adorno gives particular sharpness to the question of what is positive. What is that thing that is not subjunctive, but indicative, the good that is given already? What is the prior gift that our human acts can never catch up with? In a similar way, the question is also put in light of the touching negative theology that Luther had experienced and taught before his Reformation turning point in 1518. In his pre-Reformation days, Luther had lived a life of monastic asceticism that involved an extreme negation of worldly relations. In all seven hours of the daily office, Psalm 51 had to be prayed, and there in verse four he found the source of hatred of God[14] and uncertainty of salvation: "Against you, you alone have I sinned, and done what is evil in your sight, so that you are justified in your sentence and blameless when you pass judgment." Justification was restricted to the relation between God and the self, conceived as a negation of the self and the world; as a negative self-relation, it remained uncertain. Luther's theology at this period was one of radical denial of the world, and at the same time it was a theology of uncertainty.

In contrast, Luther's Reformation theology was one of assurance of salvation as well as a comprehensive perception of the world, not in negative, but in extremely positive terms. For faith in the promise of life through death, and the hope grounded in this promise, do not exclude the world but disclose it, and do so with incomparable breadth and depth. They do not do this, of course, in the way that a post-Christian natural theology does, as, for example, that of Hegel. For Hegel, the world and its history are transparent, and the contemplative spirit can recognize that everything "takes place rationally."[15] Faith does not enter into the whole range of nature and history speculatively. Perceiving the world in the pos-

---

14. Ps. 51:4; WA 54:185,21-28, see also Appendix, Text I; LW 34:336-37.
15. Hegel, *Die Vernunft in der Geschichte,* in *Vorlesungen über die Philosophie der Weltgeschichte,* Philosophische Bibliotek, vol. 171a, ed. J. Hoffmeister (Hamburg, Leipzig: Meiner, 1968), 28. Translated by Robert Hartman under the title *Reason in History* (New York: Liberal Arts Press, 1953).

itive way of Luther's Reformation theology does not mean to justify the world as it is. Assurance of salvation is not knowledge. Here lies the basic distinction between the theology of Luther and the philosophy of Hegel.

Assurance of Salvation Is Not Knowledge

Hegel knows, of course, just like Luther, about the misery of this world, about its injustice and the suffering in it, about its irrationality and the millions of victims of world history, of that life-and-death struggle for recognition by everyone against everyone. But he can conceive of all of this as justified and rational reality on the basis of a speculative understanding of the death of God and of the reconciliation established by that death. The power of the resurrection as "spirit" reconciles all contradictions so that Hegel can say, "What is rational is real; and what is real is rational."[16] The contemplative spirit or thought comprehends, with all that has happened in history, its own time and present in thinking and justifies them in this way. Thus thinking brings about justification, justifies all that exists including the being of God. For Hegel, it is precisely through our thoughts, by which we justify God, that God justifies *himself*, and thus already shows himself to be definitely in the right. "Reason cannot tarry at the point at which some individuals have been offended."[17] The individual in one's particularity and sensitivity is left on the garbage heap of history; the individual is refuse. Only in that the individual is a moment within the general is one's existence justified. Thus, the misery and suffering of this world are ultimately regarded as irrelevant. This contemplative theodicy supposes the painful difference between the promise of life and all that contradicts it to be already resolved. The passion of lament, which perceives this difference, dissolves

16. Hegel, *Vorrede zu den Grundlinien der Philosophie des Rechts*, vol. 7 of *Sämtliche Werke, Jubiläumsausgabe*, ed. H. Glockner (Stuttgart: Verlag frommann holzboog, 1952), 33. Translated by T. M. Knox under the title *Hegel's Philosophy of Right* (Oxford: Clarendon Press, 1942), 10.

17. Hegel, *Die Vernunft in der Geschichte*, 48. Compare this text with WA 43:481,32-35; LW 5:76 and WA 24:22,31-23,32.

and gives way to "the passionless stillness of knowledge that only thinks."[18] In such a passionless stillness of knowledge that only thinks, the inherited distinctions between the light of nature, the light of grace, and the light of glory[19] are already removed. According to Hegel, God sees himself in and through our spirit and allows us to know that all things are rational and justified.

Already Prepared

Luther clearly rejected such a contemplative theodicy, particularly in his *Bondage of the Will,* just as he rejected all forms of an active theodicy, which postulates God's righteousness against worldly experience, and finds in action an answer to the problem of theodicy. In Luther's view the righteousness and kingdom of God can never be established by human achievement. They cannot be brought about by our morality.[20] They will never be the object of a fulfillment of duty in obedience to the "categorical imperative."[21] On the contrary, they are the epitome of a categorical gift, a gift that is absolute. They come from the pure goodness of God. They are given freely out of nothing. They were already prepared long before us, prior to the whole world's foundation.[22] Luther stated this truth most impressively: "The Kingdom of God is not being prepared but has been prepared, while the sons of the Kingdom are being prepared, not preparing

18. Hegel, *Vorrede zur 2. Ausgabe der Wissenschaft der Logik,* vol. 4 of *Sämtliche Werke, Jubiläumsausgabe,* 35.

19. WA 18:785,26f.; LW 33:292. See also Appendix, Text II.

20. Even Kant says that "to found a moral people of God is therefore a task whose consummation can be looked for not from men but only from God Himself. Yet man is not entitled on this account to be idle in this business." *Religion Within the Limits of Reason Alone,* trans. Theodore M. Greene and Holt H. Hudson (New York: Harper, 1960), 92.

21. See Kant, *Grundlegung zur Metaphysik der Sitten* (1785), vol. 7 of *Werke in Zehn Bänden,* ed. Wilhelm Weischedel (Darmstadt: Wissenschaftliche Buchgesellschaft, 1983). Translated by Mary Gregor under the title *Groundwork of the Metaphysics of Morals* (New York/Cambridge, UK: Cambridge University Press, 1997). See also *Kritik der praktischen Vernunft* (1788), vol. 7 of *Werke in Zehn Bänden.* Translated by T. K. Abbott under the title *Critique of Practical Reason* (Amherst, NY: Prometheus Books, 1996).

22. Cf. Matt. 25:34 in the parable of the Last Judgment.

the Kingdom; that is to say, the Kingdom merits the sons, not the sons the Kingdom."[23]

The question of theodicy cannot be answered either actively with Kant or speculatively with Hegel. It can be resolved neither speculatively nor morally; it cannot be "resolved" in any way. We have to deal with it "practically"[24] by experiencing it in meditation (hearing and learning the Bible), in affliction, and in prayer.[25] The passive righteousness of faith does not conduct a debate *about* God and God's righteousness, as does the natural, the redeemed, or the presumably already glorified reason before its own forum. It conducts a dispute *with* God in prayer and lament.

"That God Alone Is Righteous"

The passive righteousness of faith is experienced in view of what contradicts creation, the "rent that runs from top to bottom." The door to paradise is again open. This is the climax of Luther's testimony about the Reformation turning point or breakthrough, when he learned to know the righteousness of faith. In our new nature, when that gate has been reopened, we are very different from what we were in our old nature. Nevertheless, until we die, we are still painfully related to it. We do not escape testing and temptation because of our faith. Faith is rather the courage to endure the old world and to call upon God, certain that God will hear and answer even though he may at times seem not to do so.

Luther's comprehensive and last substantive word on the question of justification is found in the concluding section of his *Bondage of the Will*.[26] This conclusion shows impressively how Luther confronts athe-

---

23. WA 18:694,26f.; LW 33:153; Cl 3:187,31-34.

24. Luther can call the experience of faith "practical," but what he has in mind transcends the schema of theory and praxis. Cf. WATR 1:72,16-24 (no. 153); LW 54:22.

25. The marks of theological existence, which are for Luther the same for every Christian, are prayer, meditation, and trial. WA 50:658,29–660,30. Cf. Bayer, *Theologie,* vol. 1 of *Handbuch Systematischer Theologie,* ed. Carl Heinz Ratschow (Gütersloh: Gütersloher Verlaghaus, 1994), 55-106.

26. WA 18:783-85; LW 33:288-92 (see Appendix, Text II).

ism. He shows plainly that although the need to explain the problem of justification in the justification dispute is important, one is not forced to speak of God in this context, all the more of the God who is concrete and tangible in the water of Baptism, in the bread and wine of the Lord's Supper, and in the words of those who speak to us in the name of Jesus, who justifies us without question or condition. When we ignore this unconditionality and try to understand the order of the world through the "light of nature" or natural reason, we want to perceive a perspicuous nexus of acts and consequences. But we will be like the friends of Job, who according to Luther, "had human and worldly concepts of God and his righteousness, as though God were like us and his laws like those of the world."[27] No less appropriate than the views of these rationalists are those of the empiricists. Luther says,

> If you respect and follow the judgment of human reason, you are bound to say either that there is no God, or that God is unjust. . . . Look at the prosperity the wicked enjoy and the adversity the good endure, and note how both proverbs and that parent of proverbs, experience, testify that the bigger the scoundrel the greater his luck. "The tents of the ungodly are at peace," says Job [Job 12:6], and Psalm 72 [73:12] complains that the sinners of the world increase in riches. Tell me, is it not in everyone's judgment most unjust that the wicked should prosper and the good suffer? But that is the way of the world. Here even the greatest minds have stumbled and fallen, denying the existence of God and imagining that all things are moved at random by blind Chance or Fortune. So, for example, did the Epicureans and Pliny; while Aristotle, in order to preserve that Supreme Being of his from unhappiness, never lets him look at anything but himself, because he thinks it would be most unpleasant for him to see so much suffering and so many injustices. The prophets, however, who did believe in God, had more temptation to regard him as unjust — Jeremiah for instance, and Job, David, Asaph and others.[28]

27. *Luthers Vorreden zur Bibel,* 60; WADB 10/I:4,8-10.
28. WA 18:784,37–785,10; LW 33:291; Cl 3:290,37.

Even the faith of the "just who live by faith" is always a faith being tested. We cannot demonstrate the goodness and love of God. Believers especially cannot set aside the question, whether God is unjust. Because God's love is never provable or free from doubt, believers live under testing and temptation. Faced with God's hiddenness, they flee for refuge to God's revealed promise, "the light of the gospel, shining only through the Word and faith."[29] Faith resists that other flight into a denial of God and into talk about blind chance[30] and fortune. It cannot accept the Aristotelian metaphysics that influenced Hegel's philosophy, with its understanding of world history as God's justification. The skepticism of faith sobers down the forceful enthusiasm that tries to harmonize reality in the concept of unity, in the monarchical principle, for the cost of this is an ignoring of the misery, injustice, and suffering of the world.[31] Luther could not agree with Aristotle or Hegel, and was of the same mind as Job and the prophets. Regarding the "question of unrighteousness in God, they too, were tempted and assaulted."

The basis and conclusion of the book of Job is simply "that God alone is righteous."[32] That is also Luther's final word in *The Bondage of the Will*. We do not see or know this; it is true only in the hope of faith. "The light of glory shows that the God whose judgment conceals an incomprehensible righteousness is of a most just and manifest righteousness. We can only believe this."[33] This "solution" to the problem does not resolve our laments. It keeps them awake and also gives us a passionate hope that in the consummation of the world, God will finally vindicate himself and answer our laments in a way that leaves no further room for testing and temptation.

---

29. WA 18:785,20; LW 33:292; Cl 3:290,8,24.

30. WA 18:706,15f.; LW 33:171; Cl 3:200,29f.

31. WATR I:57,41–58,19 (no. 135) and 73,19-32 (no. 155), opposing Aristotle's Metaphysic XII.

32. *Luthers Vorreden zur Bibel,* 60; WADB 10/I:4,17.

33. WA 18:785,35-37; LW 33:288-92; Cl 3:291,15-18.

Advent and Creation: "All Out of Pure Goodness"

In Luther, as in Job and Paul in Romans 11:33-36,[34] the hope of faith that God alone is righteous is based upon belief in God the Creator — a belief to which the passive righteousness of faith liberates us. The hope in God's eschatological advent for the whole world, for the "light of glory," turns back to creation. Its confidence lies in the efficacious Word that creates life, and grants and sustains communion. It relies upon the Word with which God called all things into their existence. The world was called into being without any worldly condition, in pure freedom and pure goodness. Creation out of nothing means that everything that is exists out of sheer gratuity, out of pure goodness.[35] "All this is done out of pure, fatherly and divine goodness and mercy, without any merit or worthiness of mine at all!" That is how Luther puts it when explaining the first article of the creed in the Small Catechism.[36] The terms "merit" and "worthiness" both belong directly to the language of the theology of justification. Yet they do not occur in the exposition of the second and third articles of the creed, only in the exposition of the first. This is a striking feature, and it indicates the breadth and depth of the justifying Word. This Word concerns not just my history but world history and the history of nature; it concerns all things.[37]

Those who live in the dispute of "justifications," asking about the ground of their own lives within this world, are told that everything is groundless and gratuitous, and they need not ground or justify themselves; it is grounded and justified only by God's free and ungrounded Word of love. Under no obligation and without any condition, God promises communion, communion through and beyond death. The justification of the ungodly, the resurrection of the dead, and creation out of nothing all happen through this promise and pledge alone. The promise of God lets us live by faith.

34. Cf. WA 18:784,11-15; LW 33:290.

35. Cf. Job 41:3 and Rom. 11:35.

36. WA 30/I:248,9-15; BSLK, 511,3-5; BC, 354-55; BC-T, 345.

37. Cf. as a counterpart to Luther's preface to his sermons on Genesis, see WA 18: 783-85; LW 33:288-292 (see Appendix, Text II), WA 24:16-24.

Appendix

Text I

This is the testimony of Luther to his discovery and experience of the "passive" righteousness of faith in the preface to the first volume of the 1545 Wittenberg edition of his Latin works. The Latin text can be found in WA 54:185,12–186,16; the English translation is from LW 34:336-37.

Meanwhile, I had already during that year returned to interpret the Psalter anew. I had confidence in the fact that I was more skilful, after I had lectured in the university on St. Paul's epistles to the Romans, to the Galatians, and the one to the Hebrews. I had indeed been captivated with an extraordinary ardor for understanding Paul in the Epistle to the Romans. But up till then it was not the cold blood about the heart, but a single word in Chapter 1 [:17], "In it the righteousness of God is revealed," that had stood in my way. For I hated that word "righteousness of God," which, according to the use and custom of all the teachers, I had been taught to understand philosophically regarding the formal or active righteousness, as they called it, with which God is righteous and punishes the unrighteous sinner.

Though I lived as a monk without reproach, I felt that I was a sinner before God with an extremely disturbed conscience. I could not believe that he was placated by my satisfaction. I did not love, yes, I hated the righteous God who punishes sinners, and secretly, if not blasphemously, certainly murmuring greatly, I was angry with God, and said, "As if, indeed, it is not enough, that miserable sinners, eternally lost through original sin, are crushed by every kind of calamity by the law of the decalogue, without having God add pain to pain by the gospel and also by the gospel threatening us with his righteousness and wrath!" Thus I raged with a fierce and troubled conscience. Nevertheless, I beat importunately upon Paul at that place, most ardently desiring to know what St. Paul wanted.

At last, by the mercy of God, meditating day and night, I gave heed to the context of the words, namely, "In it the righteousness of God is revealed, as it is written, 'He who through faith is righteous shall live.'" There I began to understand that the righteousness of God is that by which the righteous lives by a gift of God, namely by faith. And this is the meaning: the righteousness of God is revealed by the gospel, namely, the passive righteousness with which merciful God justifies us by faith, as it is written, "He who through faith is righteous shall live." Here I felt that I was altogether born again and had entered paradise itself through open gates. There a totally other face of the entire Scripture showed itself to me. Thereupon I ran through the Scriptures from memory. I also found in other terms an analogy, as, the work of God, that is, what God does in us, the power of God, with which he makes us strong, the wisdom of God, with which he makes us wise, the strength of God, the salvation of God, the glory of God.

And I extolled my sweetest word ["the righteousness of God"] with a love as great as the hatred with which I had before hated the word "righteousness of God." Thus that place in Paul was for me truly the gate to paradise.

Appendix

Text II

At the end of Luther's great work against Erasmus in 1525, *The Bondage of the Will,* the following passage can be found. The original Latin can be found in WA 18:783-85,38; the English in LW 33:288-92. A masterful exposition of this text is now available: Thomas Reinhuber, *Kämpfender Glaube. Studien zu Luthers Bekenntnis am Ende von De servo arbitrio* (Berlin/New York: de Gruyter, 2000).

For my own part, I frankly confess that even if it were possible, I should not wish to have free choice given to me, or to have anything left in my own hands by which I might strive toward salvation. For, on the one hand, I should be unable to stand firm and keep hold of it amid so many adversities and perils and so many assaults of demons, seeing that even one demon is mightier than all men, and no man at all could be saved; and on the other hand, even if there were no perils or adversities or demons, I should nevertheless have to labor under perpetual uncertainty and to fight as one beating the air, since even if I lived and worked to eternity, my conscience would never be assured and certain how much it ought to do to satisfy God. For whatever work might be accomplished, there would always remain an anxious doubt whether it pleased God or whether he required something more, as the experience of all self-justifiers proves, and as I myself learned to my bitter cost through so many years. But now, since God has taken my salvation out of my hands into his, making it depend on his choice and not mine, and has promised to save me, not by my own work or exertion but by his grace and mercy, I am assured and certain both that he is faithful and will not lie to me, and also that he is too great and powerful for any demons or any adversities to be able to break him or snatch me from him. "No one," he says, "shall snatch them out of my hand, because my Father who has given them to me is greater than all" [John 10:28f.]. So it comes about that, if not all, some and indeed many are saved, whereas by the power of free choice none at all would be saved, but all would perish together. Moreover, we are also certain and sure that we please God, not by the merit of our own working, but by the favor of his mercy promised to us,

83

and that if we do less than we should or do it badly, he does not hold this against us, but in a fatherly way pardons and corrects us. Hence the glorying of all the saints in their God.

Now, if you are disturbed by the thought that it is difficult to defend the mercy and justice of God when he damns the undeserving, that is to say, ungodly men who are what they are because they were born in ungodliness and can in no way help being and remaining ungodly and damnable, but are compelled by a necessity of nature to sin and to perish (as Paul says: "We were all children of wrath like the rest" [Eph. 2:3], since they are created so by God himself from seed corrupted by the sin of the one man Adam) — rather must God be honored and revered as supremely merciful toward those whom he justifies and saves, supremely unworthy as they are, and there must be at least some acknowledgement of his divine wisdom so that he may be believed to be righteous where he seems to us to be unjust. For if his righteousness were such that it could be judged to be righteous by human standards, it would clearly not be divine and would in no way differ from human righteousness. But since he is the one true God, and is wholly incomprehensible and inaccessible to human reason, it is proper and indeed necessary that his righteousness also should be incomprehensible, as Paul also says where he exclaims: "O the depth of the riches of the wisdom and the knowledge of God! How incomprehensible are his judgments and how unsearchable are his ways!" [Rom. 11:33] But they would not be incomprehensible if we were able in every instance to grasp how they are righteous. What is man, compared with God? How much is there within our power compared with his power? What is our strength in comparison with his resources? What is our knowledge compared with his wisdom? What is our substance over against his substance? In a word, what is our all compared with his?

If, therefore, we confess, as even nature teaches, that human power, strength, wisdom, substance, and everything we have, is simply nothing at all in comparison with divine power, strength, wisdom, knowledge, and substance, what is this perversity that makes us attack God's righteousness and judgment only, and make such claims for our own judgment as to wish to comprehend, judge, and evaluate the divine judgment? Why do we not take a similar line here too, and say, "Our judgment is nothing in comparison with the divine judgment"? Ask Reason herself whether she is not convinced and compelled to confess that she is foolish and rash in not allowing the judgment of God to be incomprehensible, when she admits that everything else divine is incomprehensible. In all other matters we grant God his divine majesty, and only in respect of his judgment are we prepared to deny it. We cannot for a while believe that he is righteous, even though he has promised us that when he reveals his glory we shall both see and feel that he has been and is righteous.

I will give an example to confirm this faith and console that evil eye which suspects God of injustice. As you can see, God so orders this corporal world in its external affairs that if you respect and follow the judgment of human reason, you are bound to say either that there is no God or that God is unjust. As the poet says: "Oft I am moved to think there are no gods!" For look at the prosperity the wicked enjoy and the adversity the good endure, and note how both proverbs and that parent of proverbs, experience, testify that the bigger the scoundrel the greater his luck. "The tents of the ungodly are at peace," says Job [Job 12:6], and Psalm 72 [73:12] complains that the sinners of the world increase in riches. Tell me, is it not in everyone's judgment most unjust that the wicked should prosper and the good suffer? But that is the way of the world. Here even the greatest minds have stumbled and fallen, denying the existence of God and imagining that all things are moved at random by blind Chance or Fortune. So, for example, did the Epicureans and Pliny; while Aristotle, in order to preserve that Supreme Being of his from unhappiness, never lets him look at anything but himself, because he thinks it would be most unpleasant for him to see so much suffering and so many injustices. The prophets, however, who did believe in God, had more temptation to regard him as unjust — Jeremiah for instance, and Job, David, Asaph and others. What do you suppose Demosthenes and Cicero thought, when after doing all they could they were rewarded with so tragic a death?

Yet all this, which looks so very like injustice in God, and which has been represented as such with arguments that no human reason or light of nature can resist, is very easily dealt with in the light of the gospel and the knowledge of grace, by which we are taught that although the ungodly flourish in their bodies, they lose their souls. In fact, this whole insoluble problem finds a quick solution in one short sentence, namely, that there is a life after this life, and whatever has not been punished and rewarded here will be punished and rewarded there, since this life is nothing but an anticipation, or rather, the beginning of the life to come.

If, therefore, the light of the gospel, shining only through the Word and faith, is so effective that this question which has been discussed in all ages and never solved is so easily settled and put aside, what do you think it will be like when the light of the Word and of faith comes to an end, and reality itself and the Divine Majesty are revealed in their own light? Do you not think that the light of glory will then with the greatest of ease be able to solve the problem that is insoluble in the light of the Word or of grace, seeing that the light of grace has so easily solved the problem that was insoluble in the light of nature?

Let us take it that there are three lights — the light of nature, the light of grace, and the light of glory, to use the common and valid distinction. By the light of nature it is an insoluble problem how it can be just that a good man should suffer and a bad man prosper; but this problem is solved by the light of grace. By the light of grace it is an insoluble problem how God can damn one who is unable by any power of his own to do anything but sin and be guilty. Here both the light of nature and the light of grace tell us that it is not the fault of the unhappy man, but of an unjust God; for they cannot judge otherwise of a God who crowns one ungodly man freely and apart from merits, yet damns another who may well be less, or at least not more, ungodly. But the light of glory tells us differently, and it will show us hereafter that the God whose judgment here is one of incomprehensible righteousness is a God of most perfect and manifest righteousness. In the meantime, we can only *believe* this, being admonished and confirmed by the example of the light of grace, which performs a similar miracle in relation to the light of nature.

Index of Names

Adorno, Theodor, 12, 73-74
Anaximander of Miletus, 5-6, 30
Aristotle, 45, 78, 79, 85
Augustine, 11, 28, 48n.

Bayer, Oswald, 4n., 23n., 27n., 40n.,
  48n., 61n., 64n., 77n.
Bengel, Johann Albrecht, 65
Bloch, Ernst, 17, 45
Bonhoeffer, Dietrich, 3, 25
Brenz, Johannes, 72n.
Büchner, Georg, 7n., 8n., 69, 70n.

Calvin, John, 23
Camus, Albert, 9n.
Cicero, 85
Clausnitzer, Tobias, 26

Demosthenes, 85
Dürer, Albrecht, 56

Engels, Friedrich, 10

Faust, 45
Fichte, Johann Gottlieb, 13
Freud, Sigmund, 16n., 17

Hamann, Johann Georg, 5n., 21n., 67
Hegel, Georg Friedrich Wilhelm, 8, 11-
  13, 24, 65, 74-77, 79

Hercules, 16
Hobbes, Thomas, 5
Hölderlin, Friedrich, 18

Jonas, Hans, 13-15

Kant, Immanuel, 8, 12-13, 16, 20-21,
  76n., 77
Kierkegaard, Søren, 27n., 65
Kleist, Heinrich von, 15-16, 19
Klepper, Jochen, 26n.

Leibniz, Gottfried W., 8-9, 11

Marcuse, Herbert, 16-17
Marx, Karl, 10n., 17-18, 45

Plato, 11, 45
Pliny, 78, 85

Sartre, Jean-Paul, 18
Schiller, Friedrich, 16
Spener, Philipp Jakob, 63

Thucydides, 4-5
Twesten, August D. C., 50n.

Weber, Max, 17, 45

Index of Biblical References